PLAYING *with* MONEY

PLAYING *with* MONEY

ROBERT BRACEY

SPINK

First edition published in Great Britain
in 2019 by Spink and Son Ltd

Copyright © Robert Bracey, 2019

A CIP catalogue record for this book is available from
the British Library

ISBN 978-1-912667-04-8

Typeset by Russ Whittle

Printed and bound in Wales by Cambrian Printers,
Aberystwyth

Spink and Son Ltd
69 Southampton Row
London WC1B 4ET

www.spinkbooks.com

CONTENTS

ACKNOWLEDGEMENTS

I should begin by thanking Tom Hockenhull, curator of modern money at the BM, who asked me to spend my weekends designing an exhibition to fill a gap in the BM's schedule, and Philip Attwood who suggested I spend my remaining spare time writing a book. Working up an exhibition on a subject an institution has not tackled before can be frustrating and difficult but it is also very rewarding.

My thanks also to Amelia Dowler who worked with me on the content and commented extensively on the text, and to Iain Birkett, Greg Szuglit, Anita Murray, Barrie Cook, and Alice-Amanda Hinton, for all of their help. Also to Emma Howard and Russell Whittle who edited and designed the book, and to the staff at the Coins & Medals department, attendees at seminars, and the design and interpretation staff of the Museum, who ensured this was fun even when it threatened to feel like a chore.

It is also important to acknowledge the many artists who helped shape the games we play, largely unknown, as publishers, who usually hold the copyright, rarely credit all of those involved in the creation of the game. Within these pages images of specific objects have been used for the purpose of comment or criticism, and the publisher of that edition has been credited.

The publishers are grateful to HarperCollins Publishers Ltd for their kind permission to reprint extracts from *Fellowship of the Ring* and *The Hobbit* by JRR Tolkien.

INTRODUCTION

"There is in a great toystore an extraordinary gaiety which makes it preferable to the finest bourgeois apartment. Is not the whole of life to be found there in miniature, and in forms far more colourful, pristine, and polished than the real thing."

Charles Baudelaire 'The Philosophy of Toys'[1]

Board games are thousands of years old and a feature of many societies. Though often played purely for entertainment they are more than simply fun. They reflect attitudes and understandings of the world, and some games are themselves models of real world activities. For example the modern game of *Chess* is derived from a fifth/sixth century AD Indian game which depicted the then current understandings of the warfare described in heroic poems like the Mahabharata. And *Chess* is not some arbitrary representation. The movement of the pieces reflects the perceived effectiveness and role of the different arms; infantry, cavalry, elephants, and chariots, of ancient Indian armies. It is the earliest military simulation, or wargame, for which records survive, and by far the most complex game known from the ancient world.

It is that idea of a game as a simulation or reflection of reality which will be explored in this book, but rather than warfare we will focus on another pervasive human experience, economics, in particular on money. Until the twentieth century board games were overwhelmingly representations of conflict, racing, hunting, or other physical pursuits. It was only in the early twentieth century that games about economics first became popular. In this book we will explore the development of those modern board games which represent money, beginning from their immediate predecessors in the late nineteenth century and

1

following that thread to the present day, and particularly from 1932 when games modelling different aspects of the economy (property, speculation, customs duties, and so on) became a regular part of the commercial games most people play.

Chapter 1 will begin in the United States, because that is the birth place of modern board games. It will examine how games, which had represented success in moral or spiritual terms, were replaced by games about material success. This sets the stage for Chapter 2, about Elizabeth Magie's *Landlord's Game*, which was the first modern game. In Chapter 3 we will look at the stock market, and how game designers have chosen to represent it throughout the twentieth century. Chapter 4 will focus on one game, *Totopoly*, first published in 1938 during a period of innovation in games, in this case representing horse-racing and gambling, one of the most popular way in which people play with money.

In the 1970s the playing of games fragmented with many different types of games appealing to smaller and smaller audiences. At the time it seemed that modern board games might disappear entirely and be replaced as entertainment by television and computers and Chapters 5 will explore the question. Chapter 6 will look at role-playing games, which came close to supplanting modern games in the 1970s and 80s, and how they represent money. The renaissance of modern board games which occurred in the 1990s was driven by innovative design from Germany, known as euro-games, and how these games develop their distinctive approach, which included a distinctive approach to money will be the subject of Chapter 7. Just one of these games, *Alhambra*, will be the subject of Chapter 8. The final Chapter 9 will look at the unintentional, and sometimes negative ways that toys and games can reflect the society they are made in, and the difficult but very interesting issues that raises.

The Book of the Exhibition

This book was written while developing a small temporary exhibition at the British Museum, called 'Playing with Money', from April to September 2019. The exhibition was an opportunity to explore ideas about how we think about money, and to display parts of the Museum's collection that are rarely seen, particularly paranumismatics (things which resemble but are not money). This book is not a catalogue of the exhibition, for example there was more in the exhibition about children's toys, and more here about the history of games, but they do share a lot in common.

A Defence

> "I assert that there exists in every State a complete ignorance about children's games—how they are of decisive importance for legislation, as determining whether the laws enacted are to be permanent or not."
>
> *Plato (Laws)*

This book resulted from an exhibition that drew heavily on the British Museum's collection of toy and game money[2]. And when I tell someone that I feel a nagging sense that I need to offer a defence, not just in the sense of why the British Museum of all places has something as trivial as game money but also a defence that games are not trivial, that they are actually quite important.

The first thing to say is that the British Museum has had a collection of toy money since the late nineteenth century. It acquired its first toy coin in 1863 and just two years later it received a representative collection of toy money when it was loaned the Bank of England's collection. The museum also has a fairly substantial collection of board games focused on money. There are educational games about the United Kingdom's transition to decimal currency in 1971 and more than one copy of *Monopoly*. The physical copy of *The Diner's Club Credit Card Game*, which was used to create the entry in the online database board gamegeek.com (an important database of games and also forum for enthusiasts) is the one in British Museum[3].

The oldest game to feature money in the British Museum is a copy of Norman Angell's *The Money Game* published in 1931. Norman Angell was the author of a hugely influential book called 'The Great Illusion' in 1913, in which he argued that advanced industrial nations could not benefit from waging war even if they were victorious. His game was designed to teach basic economic principles in the hope that greater economic literacy could underpin peaceful co-existence. He won the Nobel peace prize for his efforts in 1933.

Fig.1 'Angel of Peace', Vanity Fair portrait of Norman Angell published in 1913

In 2007 the museum began to acquire denominations sets, that is one of each money like object extracted from a game and stored, like the toy money, alongside actual coins and banknotes. Denomination sets make it easy to compare representations of money across games and over time. Storing the alongside actual money makes the relationships, and differences, more starkly apparent. Those first three sets were from 1960s versions of *Monopoly*, *Careers*, and the less well known *Go: The International Currency Game*. Since then many more have been acquired, and at the time of writing the museum has more than 600 objects from more than 80 different games.

*Fig 2 Norman Angell's **The Money Game** (J M Dent & Sons, 1928) in which players explore the concept of money supply*

I would expect the existence of such a collection to be at least be mildly surprising and could imagine at least two reasonable objections to its existence. The first objection would be that it does not belong in a museum in this way. Game money does not make much sense removed from the games themselves, and games about money belong with games that are not about money. This objection might suggest that the museum has 'decontextualised' the objects by collecting and storing them as it has[4].

The second objection might be that they do not belong in this particular museum. It would be fine in Pollock's Toy Museum or the Museum of Childhood in London, the Strong Museum of Play in the USA or the Musée Suisse du Jeu, in Switzerland, but modern games have not really earned their place alongside the Rosetta Stone, the sculptures of Benin, or the porcelain of medieval China, as pre-eminent cultural artefacts.

I would argue these objects do belong in the British Museum, alongside other contemporary objects which have always formed part of the collection. Modern games are important with interesting things to say about society, or at least I hope to show that in the chapters that follow, though I understand the objection. Putting an object in a museum always removes it from its original context but it does not obliterate context. That is simply not how museums work. What they actually do is both more interesting, and in some ways more dangerous. Museums give objects new contexts. Putting denomination sets of game money together allows you to compare them. The way game money is printed has changed, so have the designs, (as the perennial complaint about consumer goods suggests they have become smaller). It is hard to see that unless you look at denomination sets from games side by side.

Placing game money in the context of actual coins and banknotes is also revealing. Early examples of game money tend to resemble 'scrip', the locally issued paper currencies made during the American Great Depression (c.1929-1936) when problems with banks made Federal banknotes hard to get. It is only in the 1960s that game money starts to regularly look like official banknotes. In Chapter 6 we will see that representations of coins began to replace paper notes in games in the 1990s, and in Chapter 7 what the coins depicted in the game *Alhambra* are actually based on. It is hard to understand those representations except by comparing them with their real world parallels.

Fig.3 Like many other things game money has shrunk over time, examples from **Totopoly** *(Waddingtons, 1938),* **Wembley** *(Ariel, 1952),* **Executive Decision** *(Avalon Hill, 1981) and* **Maloney's Inheritance** *(Ravensburger, 1988) showing the shrinkage of paper notes*

Game money, and games, reflect real historical issues, and that is only apparent when a variety of perspectives, and contexts, are applied to its study. A museum needs that if it wants to tell stories about the past. The things people make are records of their attitudes, ideas, and beliefs. That is as true of mundane everyday objects as it is of great works of art. If museums collect only the great works they can lose the ability to tell important stories about the past, or risk distorting them. I think two parts of the British Museum's collection illustrate this very well.

Amongst the British Museum's collection of toy money is a small group of objects known as Whist Counters. They were made in the 1850s by several different manufacturers during a Victorian craze for trick-taking games which led to *Bridge.* The Whist Counters arrived in the collection between 1870 and 1906[5] when they were still everyday objects. What curators thought of them is unknown but for our purposes they are very informative. Each one is engraved with a short aphorism: 'la vie est un Jeu', 'Keep your Temper', 'No Cheating', 'Be moderate in your stakes'. The curators who collected them, largely the sort of middle-class people who played *Whist*, probably saw them as decorative truisms, but they are actually extolling the virtues of middle class gambling at exactly the moment in English history when those same middle classes were pushing for ever more draconian restrictions on the gambling of the working class (more on this in Chapter 4). A better illustration of nineteenth century middle class hypocrisy it is hard to imagine, and I did not know they existed until I chanced upon them one day while looking for early examples of toy money.

The second example illustrates how assumptions about what is 'important' or 'deserving' can distort museum collections and thus our sense of the past. The British Museum has a lot of board games, not just games that involve money, and some are quite famous, like the *Royal Game of Ur* or the Lewis Chessmen. They have been collected by different curators at different times and for different reasons. So, when I wrote this, the British Museum owned two copies of *Monopoly*, and one copy of *Risk*, but not a single example of *Diplomacy*, *Acquire* or *Settlers of Catan*. Other than these board games, the twentieth century is represented by a large collection of printed roll and move games, essentially variously decorated *Snakes and Ladders* type games, from pre-1950 Germany, and no less than sixty *Mancala* boards. *Mancala* is a simple game using stones or seeds played widely across Africa and Asia for many centuries, but the British Museum has more than sixty boards which might date to the twentieth century, probably in part because in 1997 it held an exhibition specifically on *Mancala* ('Count and Capture: Mancala game-boards').

I cannot imagine anyone seriously suggesting that *Mancala* was 30 times more important to the cultural history of the twentieth century than *Monopoly*, or that the German game industry was more culturally significant before 1950 than it was after 1979 (which will be discussed in Chapter 7). Yet that is precisely what the collection suggests. Curators in museums need to be, and are, constantly aware of what their collecting says about the past.

So yes, games and game money (including denomination sets) deserve their place in large universal museums; if anything they probably deserve more space than they get.

1.
FROM MORALITY TO ECONOMICS: THE *BOURSE* GAMES

"... as an exercise in cultural history this essay seeks to examine the significance of one type of play, the board game, as an informal mode of education and socialization, with particular emphasis on its role as a transmitter of an old American idea – the idea of success."

David Wallace Adams & Victor Edmonds, 1977

These lines appear at the beginning of an influential article in the History of Education Quarterly. The central argument of that article was two-fold, that the changing themes of board games reflected changes in how Americans conceived of success and that they also served as a mechanism for inculcating that idea of success in children. Importantly, they argued, you should not look at games to tell you about the history of games, as an end in itself, but rather to try and understand the wider society through the ways in which games reflected and shaped that society.

When they did so they found games had interesting things to say about cultural values in the USA. One of the first games to be manufactured in the United States was the *Mansions of Happiness,* credited to Anne Abbot in 1832 but actually a copy of an English game produced around 1800[6]. The games intended purpose is indicated by a short poem Abbot attached:

At this amusement each will find
A moral to improve the mind:
It gives to those their proper due,
Who various paths of vice pursue,
And shows (while vice destruction brings)That GOOD

from every Virtue springs, Be virtuous then and forward
press,
To gain the seat of HAPPINESS.

Education, to inculcate in young children appropriate moral
values, was the game's central objective. Happiness, the goal of
the game and presumably in Abbot's opinion the goal of life,
was best achieved through chastity, temperance, and gratitude.
Game's in nineteenth century America, and even into the
twentieth century, often framed success in these Christian moral
terms, but as Adams and Edmonds pointed out that was not a
constant.

By the end of the nineteenth century games began to frame
success in material terms. George Parker, the founder of the
games company Parker Brothers, designed and published his first
game in 1883. This was a card game called *Banking*[7]. In 1889 he
had added *Office Boy* to a now substantial catalogue of games.
Office Boy was played in exactly the same fashion as *Mansions of
Happiness* but now the spaces were marked with rewards such as
'Increase in Salary' and the final objective was 'Head of the Firm'
whose image looked serious rather than happy[8]. Adams and
Edmonds concluded not just that the games reflected a shift in
American ideas of how to live your life, from puritan morality to
capitalist endeavour, but that they probably helped to reinforce
and shape those changing ideas of success.

All of this requires some caveats. Firstly, these race games are a
very specific and peculiar type of board game quite different to
those many readers may have played themselves, so much so that
labelling them both with the same term is often misleading. They
are completely random, consisting of a simple path (sometimes
numbered) on which players progressed by the throw of dice, or
use of a spinning device called a teetotum (for communities in
which dice had an association with gambling). As such the novelty

of each game could only be found in the artistic presentation of the theme which was necessarily changed and reinvented on a regular basis. Secondly, there was never a point when all such games framed success in moral terms, nor a point when they all framed it in terms of material success. Moral games continued to be published into the twentieth century. No race game themed around economics survives from the nineteenth century, but the traditional card game *Commerce* (which dates to the seventeenth or eighteenth century) shows that the theme had occurred to people before the twentieth century.

Morally themed race games were themselves only a relatively recent trend. The European antecedents of these games in the eighteenth century had been produced primarily for entertainment rather than edification. The shift seems to have occurred around the beginning of the nineteenth century, at least in the United Kingdom, and was probably associated with a number of factors. Improvements in printing technologies made it possible to produce games cheaply enough for them to be seen as disposable toys for children, and the notion of 'childhood' itself as a special time with an emphasis on education became widespread. Many of these games were accompanied by lengthy text which it was intended adults would read to the children as they played.

Many historical questions about these games remain unresolved. Whether the Puritan United States or the English middleclass were more interested in race games as moral education for children is an open question. Likewise, if the trend to focusing on material success was more pronounced in the United States than other countries would be an interesting study. One thing is fairly clear, whatever theme the art and text gave to these simple printed games they were still at their core races devoid of skill. They may have been about money, but they did not simulate anything about economies. When that changed, and games began to draw inspiration from the market the effects would be far reaching, and that happened first in America.

Bourse Games

"The days of thousands of people crowded into floor pits shouting and making hand signals to execute trades has largely passed."

Gunjan Banerji, quoted in the Wall Street Journal[9]

Many of the economic games that will be discussed in the rest of this book are in some sense simulations. A simulation differs from other types of game in the intended relationship between what the game is about, the theme, and how it is played, the mechanics. In a simulation the mechanics are intended to reflect some 'reality' of the theme. For example, as *Chess* was originally conceived the chariot (what we call the rook) could move further than other pieces because in the Indian literature *Chess* was based on chariots were the most important military unit. So we can refer to it as a simulation of ancient Indian warfare, without making a judgement of how well it reflected the realities of that warfare. Of course, once the chariot was re-themed as a castle and an all-powerful queen added to the game it ceased to be a simulation of the ancient Indian warfare which had originally inspired it, or of the European warfare contemporary with those changes.

Until the early twentieth century when games made a connection between their mechanics and theme the thing being simulated was warfare, racing, or hunting. They did not try to simulate economic activity, until *Bourse[10]*, around 1903. Bourse simply means market, and it could refer in French to a conventional market, or to a stock or commodity exchange. In the nineteenth century many of the latter operated by a practice called 'open outcry'. In an 'open outcry' system each buyer or seller simply shouts what they are looking to buy or sell and their price. Other traders can take them up on the offer on a first come first served basis.

Bourse simulates this trading fairly directly. For each player in the game there was one set of cards representing a commodity or stock. All of the cards are shuffled together and dealt out to the players. The game then proceeds simultaneously with all players calling out a number, indicating the number of cards of the same commodity they would like to trade. If two players agree on a number of cards they exchange those, and the first player to get a hand consisting entirely of one commodity has cornered the market – a winning position.

A number of different commercial versions appeared in America shortly after 1900. Aside from *Bourse* itself, there was *Pit*, apparently invented by the psychic healer Edgar Cayce, *Commerce, Gavitt's Stock Exchange*, and *Panic*.[11] All seem to have been published in the space of a few years, and are very similar, but the order of publication, as it often is with board games, is hard to establish. A newspaper article published in October 1903 about the sale of Cayce's version[12], *Pit*, to the company Parker Brothers refers to *Bourse*, though it is unclear if that is the commercial game of that name or a generic name for the class of games[13]. It is possible that *Bourse* was originally a generic name, perhaps for a predecessor played with a standard deck of cards, and that the commercial games may have developed from that. As mentioned in the previous section the name of one variant, *Commerce,* had also been used for a traditional card game in which players exchange cards with a central pool or each other in order to form sets, and while the mechanics of play are very different it is not hard to see the leap from one to the other.

*Fig.4 An early edition of **Pit** (Parker Brothers, 1904), by far the most successful of the **Bourse** type games*

Whoever invented *Bourse*-type games, the long-term success of *Pit* (almost certainly due to it being taken up by Parker Brothers), suggests that economics had begun to resonate with the people who played games. The specific details of how stock and commodity markets functioned had become as much a part of American experience as hunts, wars, or races, despite stock ownership still being quite rare until the 1920s[14]. The appearance of several more stock market themed games, like *Frenzied Finance* and *Trusts and Busts*[15] which appeared in 1904 and 5 with distinct rules from the *Bourse*-type games, further indicates the appetite of a section of American consumers for this new entertainment.

Other cultural shifts in America undoubtedly played a part. To sell board games you need printing technologies that can reproduce them, and a potential audience that has the leisure time and literacy necessary to enjoy them. And to produce games that innovate you need regular game players. The vast majority of games are highly derivative, new games differing from old only in small details – as was the case with the many race type games such as *Mansions of Happiness* or *Office Boy*. Designers need the experience of novel and varied games to play in order to innovate themselves. As we shall see in the next chapter new ideas for financial games proliferated just after 1900 in America and would go on to transform how games were played. That these games focused on economics and material success reflects the profound importance those themes had to Americans at the time.

2.
THE INVENTION OF MODERN BOARD GAMES: *THE LANDLORD'S GAME*

"In truth the right to the use of land is not a joint or common right, but an equal right; the joint or common right is to rent, in the economic sense of the term. Therefore it is not necessary for the state to take land, it is only necessary for it to take rent. This taking by the commonalty of what is of common right, would of itself secure equality in what is of equal right — for since the holding of land could be profitable only to the user, there would be no inducement for any one to hold land that he could not adequately use, and monopolization being ended no one who wanted to use land would have any difficulty in finding it."

Henry George (Social reformer and campaigner)[16]

As we saw in the last chapter *Bourse* was innovative, and *Pit* was successful, but this class of games has never been influential. With the exception of a riff on *Pit* by the famous German designer Reiner Knizia called *Wheedle* in 2002[17] they have remained a footnote in board gaming history. The same cannot be said for patent 748,626 filed in the United States on 23 March 1903, which described for the first time *The Landlord's Game*. America was in the midst of a huge social and economic transformation, with the extension of stock trading, changes in working practices, and arguments raged about how best to deal with the economic world of the new century. Elizabeth Magie was one of the people deeply engaged in the arguments.

Today Elizabeth Magie is most famous for the game she designed, but in the first decade of the twentieth century she was primarily known for her radical politics. In 1906 she achieved nationwide notoriety when she placed an advert offering herself as a slave to the highest bidder. The advert was intended to draw attention to the plight of workers in the rapidly growing American cities, paid only enough to cover their basic subsistence[18].

Magie's interest in social justice and economics expressed itself most clearly through her advocacy of the theories of Henry George (1839-1897), a left-leaning New York politician and journalist, particularly his concept of a single-tax. Georgists, as his followers were known, believed that private ownership of land was deleterious to the public good. As the purchase of the land required only a one-off payment but provided a regular return ownership resulted in the enrichment of a small class of landowners and the general impoverishment of the rest of society. Magie designed *The Landlord's Game* to illustrate this central concept of Georgist thinking.

Radical 'new features of aim or rule'

"The only games that I have deliberately omitted are those of recent invention in Europe, America, and Japan which exhibit no new features of aim or rule. These are nearly always games of chance of the class I term 'race-games'; their number is great and their lives are usually short"

H.J.R Murray (Historian of Games), 1951

In order to understand just how radical Elizabeth Magie's new game was it is necessary to expand a little on what was said in the last chapter about what games looked like before 1903. To do so we will enlist the help of H.J.R. Murray, who published the first wide ranging academic treatment of board games, *A History of Board-Games other than Chess*, in 1952. Though he recorded a great many board games he was able to divide them into just five basic types: Alignment, Wargames, Hunt, Race, and Mancala. Four of these categories feature games without elements of chance, such as *Noughts and Crosses* (Alignment), *Chess* or *Go* (Wargames), the various *Mancala* games, and asymmetric games popular before the twentieth century like *Fox and Geese* (Hunt). Only the Race games, including *Snakes and Ladders* and *Backgammon*, generally involved an element of chance.

The main insight Murray affords us is how remarkably conservative these traditional games were. Not only are the range of rules involved very limited but the games are about a very limited number of topics, hunting, warfare, and racing, the last of which were adapted for moral education as described previously. There are no games about trade, or investments, or business, not to mention politics, medicine, and a host of other important human activities, all of which feature in games today.

Murray's *History of Board-Games* aims at a comprehensive treatment. However he excludes card games (such as *Whist* or *Mahjong*), most dice games, paper and pencil games (like *Battleship*[19]), and military wargames played with miniatures. In the early twentieth century 'board game' as a term had a much more limited sense than it does today. With this limit in mind Murray is quite comprehensive. He does miss a group of Chinese wargames featuring pieces of relative power. These were first adapted in the west by Hermance Edan in 1909 as *L'Attaque* and then licensed in English by Harry Gibson after the First World War. The game was to become most successful in English under the name *Stratego* (1944). Edan added a significant element of hidden information to the game, but it seems likely that had Murray not been so quick to dismiss commercial games of his own time he would have recognised not only its originality but its likely derivation from some traditional prototype[20]. His dismissal of contemporary games was dictated by a belief he expresses in his preface, quoted above, that such games added no new 'aim or rule', and repeated elsewhere in his work. This also led him to a much larger omission, in that he failed to acknowledge Magie's *Landlord's Game*.

Murray must have been aware of Magie's game in 1951, for reasons that will become apparent shortly, and the implication of his remark is that it falls into his category of race games. His race games are divided into various sub-categories, based on details of the moves that are made, the size and the shape of the board etc. His main purpose in these divisions is to trace how different games influenced each other, but they all boil down to two basic types.

In the first type of race game players progress on a board based on the throw of dice (as in *Snakes & Ladders*). These games can involve any number of players, each usually represented by a single playing piece, and vary considerably in complexity, but all are games of pure chance with no player skill involved. It is this first type that were adapted as educational games for children in the nineteenth century. The second type of race game allows the player some choice over how to move pieces based on the throw of dice. These are usually two-player (occasionally four), with each player having multiple pieces, and usually allow the capture of the opposing pieces if a piece lands on the same space. *Backgammon* is the most widely played of this type today, and involves considerable tactical skill.

Magie's *Landlord's Game* bears only the most superficial resemblance to these two types of race games. In the 1903 patent version the board is divided into forty spaces arranged in a square. Players move their piece clockwise by the throw of two dice, whose total they must accept. There is no end to the track, and players simply continue until they have completed five circuits. Once a player has complete five circuits they attain some control, being able to move clockwise or anti-clockwise as they see fit.

After moving, players must take an action based on the space on which they land. Some spaces have a player receive or pay money. In the case of the first space of the board which is marked with the politically loaded 'Labour upon Mother Earth generates Wages' a player receives money when they pass the space, even if they do not land on it.

This represents at least three new "features of rule" (to use Murray's phrase) but they are not the most radical innovation. Twenty-two spaces on the board represent land. If a player's piece finishes its move on one of these spaces they may choose to purchase the land in question (which costs between $10 and $220). Once the player owns the land, any subsequent player landing on the space must pay its owner a rent (between $1 and $22). Magie intended this rule to illustrate the Georgist philosophy that ownership of land cost nothing beyond its initial purchase and its ownership caused money to accumulate with landlords to the general harm of everyone else. It also created a radical new type of play.

In race games like *Backgammon* players decisions are mostly short term, for example will a move capture an opponent's piece or will it expose their own piece to capture on the next turn. We will call this tactical play. Strong players also look further into the future for less concrete advantages and we will call this strategic play. *Backgammon* features both but by design it emphasises the tactical, with the strategic element only emerging with long experience. In 1860 Milton Bradley, who founded one of America's earliest and most successful game companies (later known simply as MB Games) published the *Checkered Game of Life*. Writing about his game he suggested that if a player was forced into a disadvantageous move that "any such necessity can generally be traced to some false move made in the former part of the game, the effects of which could not be foreseen"[21], indicating that he intended for strategic, rather than tactical, thinking to dominate in his game. Bradley failed and play in his game is still dictated by immediate tactical concerns, but where he failed Magie succeeded.

Let us assume I have the opportunity to purchase a property for $70. Since the aim of the game is to finish with more money than the other players, in a four player game I would need other players to land on the space eight times to justify the investment[22]. Obviously they will not do that on the following one or two turns, they usually will not land on the space more than once on each circuit, so it is necessary for them to complete the circuit of 40 spaces (5-6 turns), and for this to happen at least twice. To justify the investment it is not enough to think just a few turns ahead, tactically, but necessary to think strategically about what will happened over the next ten or twenty turns on future circuits. The game uses this mechanic to simulate the more ambiguous, long-term, and strategic decisions, of property investment. Today this kind of strategic thinking is so central to family board games that we take it for granted[23], and forget that somebody had to invent it.

The Development of the Landlord's Game

Had Elizabeth Magie stopped there the Landlord's Game might simply have become a footnote in the history of board games, social reform, and economic simulation. Instead she taught it to friends and like-minded campaigners. A small number of copies were also published, though not it seems by any major manufacturer.[24]

The radical community in Arden, Delaware, a small commune founded on Georgist ideas in 1900 took the game up. The numbers on Magie's board began to be replaced by names for the property, for example, Fels Avenue probably for Fels House in Arden, George Street after Henry George[25], and so on. Scott Nearing, a radical economist took it up, and encouraged it amongst his students. And from there it gradually spread to other college campuses.

Various ideas were undoubtedly suggested by players and incorporated into the game as it was played. Today this process is referred to as play-testing and is a critical part of the development of all board games. In the early twentieth century the idea of professional games designers was still decades away. One innovation was to allow properties to be improved, and to group them into sets which gave a player an advantage if they were all owned. Cards were added which were drawn if players landed on certain spaces, and players were permitted to trade amongst themselves – adding still more 'new features of aim or rule' to the game.

In some cases the game travelled far beyond its original surroundings. In 1929 Ruth Harvey brought a copy to Atlantic City which proved a hit with her friends, and with the help of Ruth Hoskins they redesigned the board using local street names, and possibly added some additional rules for further improvements inspired by the local hotels in the seaside town. So by 1930 there were at least two distinct variants of the game circulating widely amongst enthusiastic adult players.

However, games companies were dismissive of the *Landlord's Game* when it was offered to them, which must have happened dozens of times through the 1920s[26]. It was too long, and too complicated for children. Like the game historian Murray they did not understand the game, nor did they understand that a growing number of adults were playing this board game as a regular hobby. It would need a final push to make someone desperate enough to risk the game on the open market, and that came after 1929.

The Wall Street Crash and the Great Depression

On 29 October 1929 the value of shares traded on the New York Stock Exchange, as represented by the Dow index, fell 12%. The crash came after several days of panic which the banks had failed to contain. Realising that speculating had created a dangerous bubble holders of shares then sought to dispose of them at any price. Black Tuesday as it is known is often seen as the beginning of the Great Depression. The Depression resulted in falling American standards of living, a massive rise in unemployment, and in many cases the freezing of bank accounts. People's money, if they had any, became locked up inside banks too frightened to allow withdrawals for fear of a 'run' that would destroy their business. Many towns took to issuing pieces of paper guaranteed against the federal bank notes people could not access, known as 'scrip'.

In 1932 George Layman managed to convince a company, Knapp Electric, to publish the most popular of the *Landlord's Game* variants under the title *Finance*. With it they printed game money which resembled far more closely the familiar scrip of the Depression than it did any federal banknote. Layman did not know Magie directly but had learnt the game in college in the mid 1920s. It was an immediate success. As the Depression began to reverse in 1933 and household incomes started to rise, *Finance* became one of the country's best selling games.

In 1935 Layman was approached by the games company Parker Brothers. They had recently acquired another variant of the game, the one developed in Atlantic City, and were marketing it under the popular name Layman had known it by at college, *Monopoly*. The new head of the company, Robert Barton, believed in a corporate folk wisdom that Parker Brothers had failed to capitalise fully on previous gaming trends (particularly

Tiddlywinks, Mahjong, and *Table Tennis*) because competitors had been able to market rival versions. He was therefore seeking to buy out any potential competitor. Layman and Knapp sold their rights and Parker Brothers continued to sell a revised version of the game, called *Finance & Fortune,* until the 1970s. Parker Brothers went on to strike deals with Milton Bradley over their version, *Easy Money,* and settled with others, such as the maker of *Inflation.* Pretty soon Robert Barton had what he wanted, a monopoly on *Monopoly,* and with it the most successful board game of all time.

Elizabeth Magie's invention of *The Landlord's Game* would be relatively easy to miss as it was played by only a modest number of players in America, as *Monopoly* it became a world-wide phenomenon in the 1930s, and the board game historian Murray must have been aware of her game. Perhaps his conviction that contemporary games were all simple race games held so strong he never actually looked at it. Though Magie never succeeded in making Henry George's ideas widely acceptable she did succeed in transforming the nature of board games, creating something simple enough for children to play but challenging enough for adults, from which all modern family board games derive, and the hobby that accompanies it. It inspired other designers and companies throughout the late 1930s and into the 1950s. The famous game designer Sid Sackson (we will have more to say about him later) listed it amongst his three favourite childhood toys, and recognised its innovative qualities.[27] Though as we will see it is not an uncontroversial legacy.

How do we know so much about the history of Monopoly?

"If buyers wish to be snobs the law will protect them in their snobbery"

Judge Learned Hand (on the subject of Trademarks)

*Fig.5 Money from the revised version of **Finance** published by Parker Brothers in the late 1930s. This version retained the older street names pre-Atlantic City locations and the scrip-like appearance of the notes.*

I am a fair weather cyclist and faced with a sudden shower will retire to a coffee shop. It was under such circumstances that I chanced on one of Hasbro's 'nostalgia' publications of *Monopoly*. Since acquiring Parker Brothers in 1991 Hasbro has created a variety of these sets to allow players to 'Travel back through time and play the fast-dealing property trading game with its original designs!' as one box puts it.

The 2003 edition I was looking at was one of those. It came in a nice wooden box never actually used for historical versions of the game, and though based on the English version produced by Waddington's used the Parker Brothers logo. Although the buildings inside were wooden the money was modelled on the sets of the 1960s and 70s which used plastic buildings, not the earlier designs which prominently featured patent numbers, and it had definitely shrunk. All of this should probably have prepared me for the text on the outside of the box, which read:

"Germantown, Pennsylvania, 1930. It was the Depression and Charles B. Darrow, an unemployed salesman, was looking for affordable entertainment for his family and friends. Remembering past holiday visits to the seaside resort of Atlantic City, New Jersey, he devised a game using the city's street names and railroads. The game caught on rapidly among his friends and neighbours. Darrow knew he had a hit, and he started making game sets and selling them to local department stores. By 1934, Monopoly had taken off like a freight train. Darrow couldn't keep up with production, so he took his idea to Parker Brothers."

Now unless you skipped ahead to this section you are probably wondering why that account of *Monopoly's* creation bears no resemblance to the one I just gave. You might even have heard that account before; Parker Brothers spent a lot of money promoting it. In a generous moment you might consider the story a concoction, much like the game I was examining, evoking nostalgia but not actually true in any of the details. Others have been less generous and that false story came back to haunt Parker Brothers in a court case that revealed a lot about board game history and would go on to change US law.

In 1973 an economist called Ralph Anspach published a game called *Anti-Monopoly*. I played it in the early 1980s with family, and it is a fairly dull and unimaginative modification of *Monopoly*. Despite Robert Barton's attempts to establish near total control over Parker Brother's best selling game many people made copies, which were more or less derivative. Some, like the *Stock Market Game* in the 1960s basically just changed the labels on cards and board, others like the Turkish game *Hepsi Benim* altered map and rules to reflect local interests, much as players had in the 1920s. Anspach took the latter route, encouraging the players to break up rather than establish monopolies. Like many players in the 1970s he misunderstood the game as promotion rather than critique of its subject[28].

What Anspach appeared to realise was that success did not come from the quality of the game. Magie's design had been breathtakingly new in 1903. Even when *Finance* was published in 1932 most people had never played anything like it. By 1960 family board games had become a routine part of many families play, and games like *Buccaneer* (1938), *Scrabble* (1948), *Cluedo*

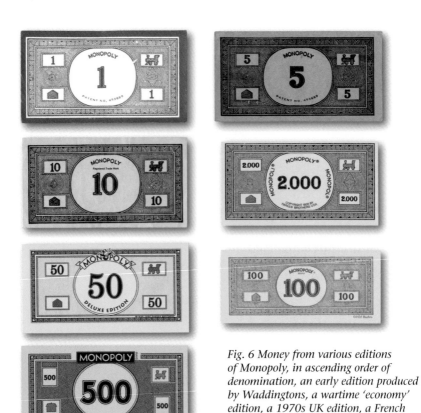

Fig. 6 Money from various editions of Monopoly, in ascending order of denomination, an early edition produced by Waddingtons, a wartime 'economy' edition, a 1970s UK edition, a French edition from 1984, US deluxe edition from 1995, a 2003 'nostalgia' edition, and a 2008 Zurich edition

(1949), *Risk* (1957), *Diplomacy* (1959), and *Formula 1* (1962) had further innovated – *Monopoly* was no longer a radical newcomer, it was now the establishment. Real value lay in the brand that Parker Brothers had built in that early period before time and imitation had robbed the *Landlord's Game* variants of their originality. So though Anspach had a workable alternative title for his game, *Bust the Trust*, he ultimately used a variation on *Monopoly* instead – both *Bust the Trust* and *Monopoly*. Anspach would subsequently claim that he was not motivated by using

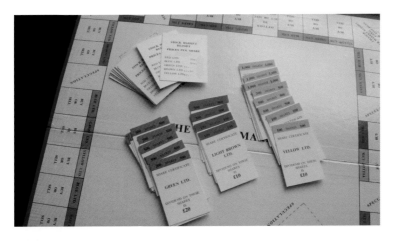

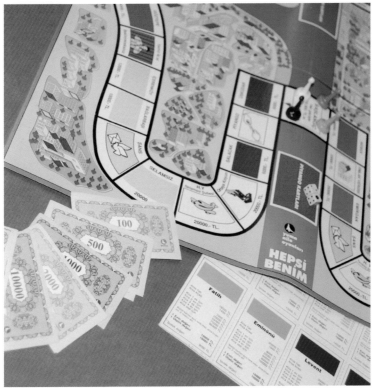

Fig.7 The **Stock Market Game** (Specialist Games Company, 1963 and **Hepsi Benim** (Yuma) are amongst the many derivatives of Monopoly published in the last 80 years.

Parker Brother's brand to sell his game, even writing a lengthy book to defend himself from the charge.

Parker Brother's were not happy and wrote to Anspach insisting he stop selling the game under that name. They held a trade mark on the name *Monopoly* and they felt that *Anti-Monopoly* was too obviously trying to benefit from their own hard work. The public benefit justification of trade marks is that it protects consumers from being tricked into buying inferior or different products though as the quote from the aptly named Judge Learned Hand suggests there has always been some discomfort about what trademarks actually do in practice.

When Anspach chose the name he believed Parker Brothers had a legitimate trade mark, and this should have been a very simple case. Anspach had a stroke of luck and discovered that the story Parker Brothers told about the game (the one on that 2003 box I looked at) was not true. Game historians have always basically known that the Parker Brother's story was not true because Magie's 1903 patent was a matter of public record, but now Anspach and his legal team began to dig. And the dispositions they took from numerous people who had played the game before Parker Brother's published their first set in 1935 went on to form the nucleus of an oral history on which I drew for the account above.

Charles Darrow had learnt the game from an old school friend of his wife, who played with one of the Atlantic City boards. He had copies made and began to sell them, but they were just copies. Darrow had not invented any of it, even faithfully reproducing spelling mistakes on the board (Marvin Gardens in Atlantic City is spelt 'Marven' in the game). Parker Brothers knew this, they had seen the earlier versions by Magie, and they knew *Finance* preceded it onto the market. Starting in 1974 Anspach entered into a long legal dispute with the owners of Parker Brothers, General Mills Inc, which ultimately ended with his victory in 1983. The trademark, along with all of the apparent legal protection for the game had been swept away.

Before you get any ideas you are going to make your own millions by printing *Monopoly* sets think again. Lawyers were pretty unhappy with the legal decision. They thought the courts had got it wrong. Businesses were very unhappy with the decision. If one of the world's most famous trademarks could be swept away like that what about their own. The government of the United States stepped into the fray and in 1984 the Trademark Clarification Act was passed into law,[29] effectively over-turning the decision. Today those responsible for monitoring trademarks continue to accept Hasbo's claims to own a relatively far reaching trademark around the game. For example claims by Hasbro that using the suffix '–opoly' in a game title infringes their rights have been recently upheld.[30]

Protected by nothing less than the power of the US government it is not clear why Hasbro continue to promote a story they know is untrue. It is possible of course that they consider the Charles Darrow story as much a nostalgic fiction as the retro versions of their own game, a Ronald McDonald sort of character. There are certainly no straightforward bad guys in the original story; Darrow was trying to care for a disabled child; Barton was trying to save a company the Depression had brought close to bankruptcy. Even so, in 2019, it is surprising that a major international company spends its money giving credit for the work of an early feminist and female inventor to a man.

Final Words

> "Board game enthusiasts don't usually play Monopoly any more. Personally, I don't really have a problem with it, it's just that there are much better games available. A lot of modern board game players certainly do have a problem with it though. I get the feeling that some of them would rather play one of Jigsaw's games from the Saw movies than play Monopoly."
>
> *Steve Dee (board games writer)[31]*

The *Monopoly* brand has come to transcend the game itself. Today *Monopoly* sets based on popular franchises, like Marvel comic books or Star Wars, are collected rather than played. And Hasbro cares just enough about Star Wars fans to use a franchise appropriate Imperial alphabet on the bank notes, but not quite enough to check them properly for typos.

Teachers use the game to illustrate social inequality, and psychologists to measure how people behave differently in proximity to money[32]. *Monopoly* has become synonymous with our everyday understandings of money. Ironically *Monopoly* has also become for modern board gamers a symbolic example of the inferiority of mass-market children's games (despite being played almost exclusively by adults before 1935). In the 1990s the tastes

*Fig.8 Imperial script on notes from the 1996 Star Wars edition of **Monopoly** (Hasbro), with 'credit' misspelt 'crpdit' in the inset circle, and the 2012 Star Wars edition of **Operation** (Hasbro), with the value incorrectly written as 'one hundred'.*

of games designers and players were transformed by a new type of game, usually referred to as 'euro games' or simply 'euros'. Commentators, often unaware of the history of the games, saw these games as a dramatic break, rather than a development of older games, and *Monopoly* became the exemplar for what these games were not. It is a story we will return to in Chapter 7. In the early 1930s, however, *Monopoly* ushered in a period of rapid innovation and an increasing interest, and willingness to publish, games about money.

3.
PLAYING THE MARKETS: FROM
STOCK TICKER TO *BLACK FRIDAY*

"Popular attitudes toward the market in the late nineteenth
and early twentieth centuries ... inherited and built upon
a centuries old tradition of Anglo-American thought. The
growth of the market and the conduct of speculators
around the turn of the century may have triggered our
current schemes of regulation, but behind that trigger lay
hundreds of years of preparation"

Stuart Banner Legal Historian[33]

In the last chapter we looked at just one game, about the person
who made it and the consequences it had. This will be a very
different sort of chapter. Most modern board games did not
sell millions of copies, or become iconic brands, and very few
resulted in legal action with substantial ramifications for US
law. So the game itself is often all the evidence available, while
the story of its creation is locked away in family archives, if it
survives at all. This is especially true of modern games before the
1990s whose publishers rarely credited the designers. But we can
still see something of how games reflect changing attitudes by
comparing how they handled the same themes and mechanics.
In this case those games which over the last hundred years have
represented the stock market.

With the success of *Monopoly* as a property investing game it
must have seemed a natural extension to make games about
stock market speculation, and there are a lot of games that copy
the structure and details of *Monopoly* but substitute stocks for
property. Parker Brother's released one, called *Bull & Bears* in 1936,
just a year after they got into the market for modern board games.

Fig.9 Unsure of how to approach the new market for games in the 1930s some publisher's tried marketing the products as 'designer games' , though in this case Charles Darrow had little to do with the production of **Bulls & Bears** (Parker Brothers, 1936)

When players land on certain spaces they are obligated to buy or sell stock, and/or receive dividends. Once a player has acquired a certain amount of stock other players are obligated to pay them when landing on certain spaces. In terms of rules, tactics, or strategy, (the mechanics) the game adds nothing new to *Monopoly*, though of course the theme is a novel one. This was the same commercial route which publishers' had adopted with children's' race games since the late seventeenth century. Imitation would eventually re-assert itself as a dominant commercial practice in in the 1970s but was broadly unsuccessful from the late 1930s to the 1950s. During that period consumers showed a marked preference for games with either innovative mechanics (*Cluedo*, *Scrabble*, *Risk*) or which used the recent mechanical innovations in previously untried ways (see chapter 4 on *Totopoly*).

This chapter will be concerned with an innovation in stock market games which has both a thematic and mechanical element – the price track. As we saw in chapter 1 the *Bourse* games, which simulated the noisy atmosphere of a trading floor, originated at about the same time that Magie first worked out her ideas. And they were not alone, a series of games themed around the stock market appeared in the early twentieth century. Many of them are still traceable in patent applications even if published copies do not survive[34]. The most common type involved a spinner, which could be flicked to point to one of a huge number of spaces around the edge of the board, indicating whether the player was to buy or sell, which stocks, and the value. These first games lacked a memory; a way to ensure that the price on this turn (at which a player might buy stock) had some relation to the price on the next turn (at which the player could sell), as well as much in the way of skill. The price track was the solution to that problem. Price tracks are simple boards laid between the players, initially with columns for each stock or commodity, where the row indicates the current price, and they have persisted with only minor modifications since they were first used in the 1930s.

This chapter will focus specifically on those stock market games which use a price track, and how their simulation of the market changes over time.

Classifying games is notoriously difficult, in part because it is the work of only a few moments to invent a counter-example to any scheme. It becomes a little easier when looking at games historically because the range of games made and played in any period was always very limited and distinct trends are often apparent in hindsight. I will suggest in this chapter that those games themed around the stock market which feature a price track form a distinct group historically and that they can be further subdivided into what might be labelled punt, insider, investment, and crash games. Each of these sub-divisions focus on particular mechanics (odds generated by dice; hidden

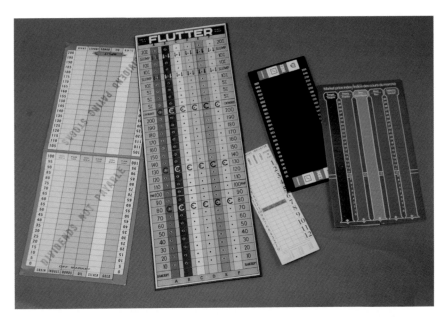

Fig.10 A variety of price tracks from stock market games, left to right, **Stock Ticker**
(Copp Clark, 1937), Flutter (Spear's, 1950), Stocks and Shares (Pepys, 1960), Broker
(Ravensburger 1971, first published 1961), and Speculate (Waddingtons, 1972)

information; sub-games; dependent probabilities and limited
actions) and emphasise different elements or interpretations
of the stock market (speculation as gambling; insider trading;
sources of capitalisation for larger enterprises; and bubbles and
crashes). These four subdivisions represent broad trends in the
design of stock market games, which very roughly followed each
other in chronological succession. They will be examined in turn
below. The divisions partly reflect periods of innovation in board
game design (from the 1930s to the early 1970s, and in the 1990s)
but also how popular understandings of stock markets changed
in the twentieth century.

We do not know how much a games simulation affects the
players understanding of the thing being simulated. There is
no doubt that the ways in which stock market games shape our

understanding of actual stock markets is extremely complicated, especially for those of us with no practical experience of the reality. The question is really for psychologists but they have by and large focused exclusively on traditional games and on theories of learning[35]. However, Stuart Banner, quoted above, has argued that legal regulation often depends on popular attitudes and understandings. In the case of the seventeenth and eighteenth century he looked to poetry and plays, popular entertainment which might reflect or shape that attitudes. Today we might imagine games having a similar role.

Take a Punt

> "Wall Street's crime, in the eyes of its classic enemies, was less its power than its morals. And the centre of immorality was not the banks but the stock market. It was on the stock market that men gambled not alone with their own money but with the wealth of the country."
>
> *John Kenneth Galbraith, economist, 1954*[36]

Though today stock exchanges are associated with grand buildings whose neo-classical stone facades project an image of respectable stability that is in fact a very recent innovation. The first stock exchange, founded in Amsterdam in 1602 to trade in the stock the Dutch East India Company, had its own building[37] but in most cities, stocks were traded in coffee shops and on street corners. Only in the nineteenth century, London in 1801, Paris after 1813, New York in 1817, and Chicago in 1882, did traders move into premises designed for the purpose, and even in New York many stocks continued to be traded on the street into the early twentieth century in what was known as the curb market. For many, trading in stocks looked no different to street betting and some practices, such as options, were seen as wagers even by insiders.[38]

As share ownership expanded, especially after the First World War,[39] and ordinary lives were impacted by the fortunes of railway or utilities companies on the stock market, it became apparent to the regulated exchanges that they had an image problem. Options, where a contract is made to buy or sell stock without necessarily owning the stock, in order to profit from future changes in prices, were widely viewed as a form of gambling, and the general public saw speculation in the same vein. Exchanges tried to educate the public about the benefits of stock markets, and to shut down poorly regulated 'bucket shops', as well as to remove any whiff of gambling from the exchanges themselves.[40]

The board game *Flutter*, first published in 1950, makes the popular understanding of stock markets explicit in the title but the mechanics of earlier games also evoked gambling. *Stock Ticker,* published in 1937[41], is driven by simple calculation of odds, and the spinner-based predecessors of these games did not simply resemble roulette, they played like it with the players' fortunes determined entirely by random chance. Overwhelmingly before 1960 stock market games presented the routine activity of the exchange, buying and selling, as little more than a wager, or a flutter on the horses.

As a game *Flutter* is undoubtedly the most interesting of these early punt games. On the price track there are six columns, each representing a market sector for a different commodity. The current value of each commodity is marked with a peg (the base peg), and it is at this price plus a fee that the players buy. The second peg of each commodity is moved by the throw of dice (one of which nominates the commodity, the other indicates how far the peg advances). When a peg reaches the end of the track dividends are paid out based on the positions of the travelling pegs, and the game resets for another round, with the travelling peg returned to the same position as the base

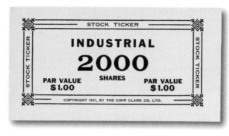

Fig.11 Money and share certificates from Stock Ticker (Copp Clark, 1937) and Flutter (Spear's, 1950). Shares are usually variations on the paper money designs rather than attempts to reflect actual certificates, which were likely unfamiliar to the majority of players.

peg. Mechanically *Flutter* is clearly based on traditional horse racing games, in which players rolled a die to decide which horse moves.

In *Flutter* wagering is made more interesting because players are allowed to purchase their shares at any time. Obviously, a commodity whose travelling peg is closer to the top of the chart is more likely to finish in a position that pays a divided. If a player waits before buying they have more information, but they also run the risk that the race will end before their next chance to buy.

Game dynamics in *Camel Up*

As well as their mechanics and themes it is possible to think of games in terms of their dynamic – the kinds of decisions players make. *Camel Up* is a modern game themed around a series of stages in a camel race. In each round players' either roll for the movement of the competing camels, thus gaining information on the likely outcome of this stage of the race, or place bets on which camel will finish first. If a player waits before placing a bet they will have more information, but as later bets get worse odds they run the risk of missing out if they wait too long – the same dynamic as *Flutter*, but with camels substituted for stock.

Fig.12 Coins as depicted in the game Camel Up (Pegasus, 2014)

By representing stock markets with simple throws of the dice, in which the only skill was assessing odds, and which evoked roulette, wagers, or horse racing, the games reflect a widespread ambivalence towards the stock market. That ambivalence remained even as designers tried to create more strategic stock market games.

Insider Trading

"The SEC is most successful, has been in the area of policing and the area of confidence and honesty in the markets, the area of insider trading. There they shine."

Lee Pickard SEC
(Securities and Exchange Commission) employee[42]

In 1961 the Spencer-Murray Corporation published a game called *Broker*. The game is also known as *Börsenspiel* and was published for many years by the German manufacturer Ravensburger from 1968. Players buy and sell shares in order to increase their initial capital from a selection of four different stocks whose prices are recorded on a price track essentially identical with that used in earlier games like *Stock Ticker* or *Flutter*.

Where *Broker* differs is in how the price of the shares is determined. On each player's turn they must play a card which will alter at least two of the stocks. This is a similar mechanic to that used in an older game rereleased in 1960, *Stocks & Shares* (originally called *Win-a-Lot*) but the details vary. In *Broker* players each receive fifteen cards and must play one on their turn. In *Stocks & Shares* each player is given one card at the start of each round and the effect of all player's cards are resolved at the end, with players trading in between. In both cases the main difference with earlier games is that information about the changes in price are not public, each player has some amount of 'insider' knowledge about future prices not available to other players.

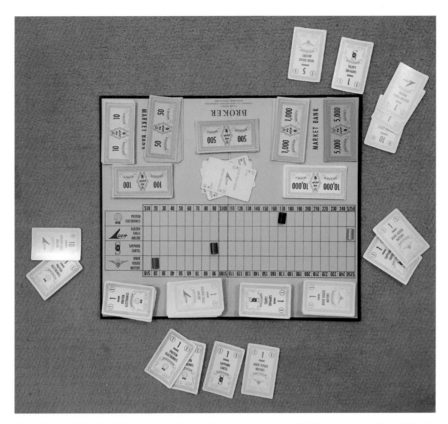

Fig.13 An original edition copy of Broker (Spencer-Murray, 1961), courtesy of Iain Birkett

In mechanical terms the addition of insider information opens up a variety of additional possibilities for bluffing, inference, card counting, and in *Broker's* case strategic planning. As each player plays all fifteen of their cards, over fifteen rounds, they can plan for stock movements many rounds into the future. Thematically inside information is also interesting because real world stock markets work that way, with those possessing inside information about a company's fortunes using that to enrich themselves, or at least they did in America until 1961.

There is no formal definition of insider trading in US law, just a complex mixture of rules and legal cases, in large part overseen and enforced by the Securities and Exchange Commission (SEC). Though the supreme court had ruled in principle that insider trading was illegal in 1909[43] and the SEC had been given powers to tackle it when it was founded in 1934 in practice no actual cases were brought. No laws would be changed until the 1980s but the culture of enforcement shifted in 1961, the year *Broker* was published[44]. Just a few years later the SEC would pursue the high-profile Texas Gulf Sulphur case.

Texas Gulf Sulphur had received survey results indicating a particularly rich find of mineral deposits, which they had initially publicly denied. Before releasing the news of the find several employees purchased stock in the company and subsequently profited from the rise in prices. Those involved were pursued vigorously by the SEC and forced to return the money they had made. In the process it kicked off a debate, about the merits of regulating insider trading which continues today. For those in favour of regulation insider trading was a simple moral question:

> "*Fortune Magazine* ran an article called the *Unwinnable War* about insider trading. It's a topic that's interesting because everyone understands lying, cheating, and stealing. While Enron and World Com have received a lot of publicity, all that most people can tell you is that there was wrongdoing in accounting and mischief of that kind that constituted illegalities, whereas as to an insider trading case, most people can explain to you what went on."
>
> *John Fedders (SEC Enforcement Division)*[45]

SEC officers had come to see insider trading in moral terms, in terms of 'honesty' or 'cheating' and expected the public to agree with them. SEC employees tend to explain this in terms of legal frameworks, but the frequent use of morally loaded terms indicates perceptions of morality helped to drive enforcement.

That is indicated by the fact that no law had actually changed, and when a court did rule against the SEC they simply sought new legal interpretations to pursue the same cases rather than rethinking whether they should[46]. At the same time there was an awareness that many economists and those in the financial industry did not agree with the pursuit of insider trading.

> "I remember John Shad [Chairman of the SEC, 1981-87] and I had lunch in New York with a couple of the senior people from the *Wall Street Journal* just to try to convince them that insider trading was a bad thing and that our spending our resources on this was a good thing for the markets, and they weren't buying it."
>
> *Gary Lynch of the SEC*[47]

The insiders who had benefited at Texas Gulf Sulphur commissioned a historian to write an entire book to set the record straight[48] and counter what they perceived as an injustice and a slight on their character. The economist Henry Manne[49] developed theoretical defences of insider trading, suggesting amongst other things that it helped to protect the market from sharp shocks. That remains a widely held opinion amongst economists, and many historical studies of markets have focused on demonstrating that insider activity was not harmful, perhaps even beneficial, and rarely (in the past) considered unethical.[50]

Does *Broker* take a stand in this debate? Are we to understand the game as an indictment of insider trading or as an endorsement? The republication by Ravensburger, after 1968, implies it was at least resonant. That publication coincided with a wide-ranging review of the German securities markets, partly motivated by public concerns.[51] This led to new rules restricting insider trading, though these were rarely enforced. The game is unusual amongst Ravensburger's catalogue, both because they tended to eschew financial games and because it was sponsored. In German editions of the game (but not the original American edition) the

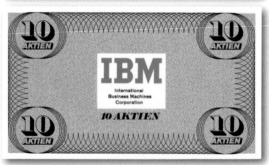

*Fig.14 Share certificates with logos for Deutsche Bank, IBM, Seimans, and British Petroleum from an early 1970s German edition of **Börsenspiel** (Ravensburger)*

four sets of stock are represented by the logos of actual German or international companies, including major financial institutions like Deutsche Bank, who presumably might be embarrassed by an association with insider trading.

Ravensburger specifically chose to license a game that represented insider trading at a moment of ambivalent or negative public attitudes to the practice, and which itself had been first released in the context of the beginnings of active regulation in America. It is hard to believe that no-one saw this as a negative commentary on the practice, but it seems unlikely institutions like Deutsche Bank would have allowed their logos to appear prominently if they had shared that perception.

There is an ambiguity in any game's simulation of a real-world phenomenon that allows different audiences to read it in different ways. We saw this in chapter 2, the *Landlord's Game* was intended as a damning indictment of private property but came to be viewed within a few generations as actively promoting capitalism. A similar fate befell some of *Broker's* contemporaries. The game *Ratrace* was invented in 1965 and is clearly satirising the explosion in US consumer credit and class divisions. It is a simple family game won by the first player to earn a million. Players earn more money by completing circuits of the board in 'middle class' or 'high society' than they do at the start in 'working class', but to move up they must acquire consumer goods which they cannot afford. Players are encouraged to buy these unaffordable status symbols on their credit cards and hope they do not land on 'credit due'. The satire extends to representing the players with plastic rats, yet a Marxist writer could within a decade assume that the game was promoting and endorsing the very thing it was attacking.[52] The lesson seems to be that games tend to be understood as normalising the dominant attitudes of the society in which they operate, and that victory conditions tend to endorse the behaviours they encourage. Whatever its original intent did *Broker* serve to endorse a reluctance in Germany to

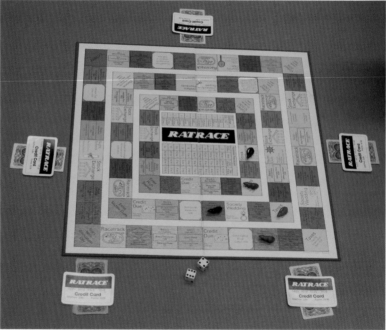

Fig.15 The Game Ratrace (Waddingtons, 1984; first published 1967) is not subtle in its satire, representing the players as plastic rats desperate not to land on 'Credit Due'

regulate insider trading?

Of course, *Broker* is not the only insider style game, and some at least were made by people who might be considered 'insiders'. In 1972 Waddingtons published a game called *Speculate*, designed by a former South African merchant banker,[53] Graeme Levin. In *Speculate* players hold a hand of three cards on each turn, playing one at the beginning and one at the end of the market. An unusual feature of this as a game is that most of the buying and selling is intended to take place directly between the players.

The claim in *Speculate* that 'this is a game based firmly on the characteristics of dealings in stocks and shares' is also echoed in another insider style game, *Stockmarket!*, published in 1987. *Stockmarket!* derives its central mechanic from the Pepys game *Stocks and Shares*. Players are dealt a hand of cards at the beginning of each round which indicate price changes. Everyone buys and sells shares before the hands are revealed and the price changes applied. Again, as with all of these games prices are adjusted, and player's trade, on the basis of non-public information, so this is clearly insider trading. *Stockmarket!* is a game that chooses to simulate the stock market solely by reference to one of its most controversial aspects. Yet the rules state: 'STOCKMARKET! is modelled on the London Stockmarket and accurately reflects all the major aspects of modern share dealing'. Not only that but the game uses the names of real companies, including at least one bank NatWest (now part of HSBC); it also appears to have been actively endorsed by the London Stock Exchange; and was used in schools as part of competitions for actively sponsored programs.[54] The games paper money, referred to as 'promissory notes' in the rules and resembling cheques, carry on them the phrase 'my word is my bond'[55] which seems to elevate the games claim from 'accurately reflects' to morally endorsing stock market practices.

Ultimately the questions around these games are not easily

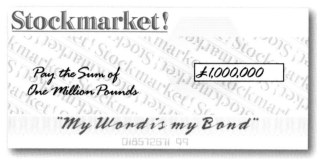

Fig.16 *The currency used for* **Stockmarket!** *(Jordans, 1987) carries the morally loaded stock exchange phrase 'my word is my bond'.*

answered. Do games tend to promote whatever behaviour the mechanics require for victory? And if they do does any level of satire or critique vanish with even a modest passage of time? It remains an open question what the designers of *Broker* actually thought they were doing, but its publication history shows an awareness and degree of response to insider trading as a stock market practice in the 1960s, even if it remains unclear how designers, publishers, sponsors, and ultimately players understood that.

A Quick Aside on Sid Sackson

"I also tried to get a favourable blurb on the game from Sid Sackson, who is a kind of Babe Ruth of the games world. Sid is the creator of Acquire and about forty other games. Anyone who knows games knows Sid, at least by reputation. If he liked it, really liked it, news of it would get out to games people everywhere"

Bertell Ollman[56]

Sid Sackson's reputation is all the more remarkable for the fact that his name does not appear anywhere on the original edition of his most famous game, *Acquire*. Games companies largely sold games by brand, in this case the 3M bookshelf games. *Acquire* was published in 1964[57] shortly after 3M had made the decision to begin its own line of games. These games were produced in boxes sized for a bookshelf and designed in sombre colours to appeal primarily to adults. They would continue to publish these and a variety of sports board games until 1975 when the general downturn in the market for modern board games (see chapter 5) led them to sell the line to the wargames company Avalon Hill. While many of the 3M games have disappeared into obscurity *Acquire* has never been out of print and remains a highly regarded game.

Sid Sackson had grown up with *Monopoly*, which he ranked among his favourite childhood games[58]. He recognised as a designer that *The Landlord's Game* had innovated 'what turned out to be one of the most important game ideas of the century, that of ownership of the board by the players'[59] and developed a game, called *Property*, inspired by this observation on the original *Landlord's Game*. In that game pairs of cards are played which give grid co-ordinates for the board, resulting in the player paying rent, purchasing or 'mortgaging' the space. As this suggests Sackson's design philosophy often focused on stripping a game to its essentials.[60] The rules of *Property* here are more streamlined and significantly shorter than the game which inspired it and there are no exceptions or information to look up. The other change, replacing dice with cards, changes the way the probabilities in the game work[61]. Both are shifts, simple rules and dependent probabilities, which heavily influenced some German designers in the late 1980s and led to the critical success of what are called euro-games (see chapter 7). In many ways Sackson's influence is as great on his successors as *Monopoly* was on him.

Acquire is not, in the sense being used here, a stock market game. Each turn a player must cover one space on the board with a tile, the choice being limited as each tile is marked with the grid co-ordinate it must be placed at (there is clearly mutual influence on *Property*). If two tiles are placed adjacent to each other they form a hotel chain. There are seven possible hotel chains and players may buy up to three shares in them each turn. The value of the chain's shares is determined by the number of connected tiles in the chain, but players cannot sell freely and share prices only go up.

Acquire's central mechanic is majority control. When two hotel chains meet, the larger absorbs the smaller. The player with the most shares in the smaller chain receives a bonus payment, and any player with shares may sell them. Being in this position is critical because without receiving money from early and mid-game mergers players will run out of cash and soon fall behind.

Several of 3M's games included a financial component and like a number of companies they created a standard design of paper money. An interesting aspect of this is that the money resembles US notes, including caricatures of various presidents. MB games also adopted the practice on the hundredth anniversary of their first game, in 1960, and placed a portrait of their founder in the centre. The potential discomfort of imitating real money is indicated by the numerous disclaimers on the MB notes. As discussed in chapter 2 the money in the first modern board games had resembled the unofficial 'scrip' currencies used during the depression – likely an association that had long since faded from the minds of players by the 1960s.

The simple and elegant design philosophy of *Acquire* would achieve its moment of ascendency in the late 1990s, but before that there would be a fracturing in the English speaking industry that would come close to ending the modern board game entirely. Sid Sackson's games came at the end of the period of innovation that had begun in the 1930s, and by the 1970s games playable by a family but challenging for adults were being displaced. For

Fig.17 A game of Acquire (3M, 1964) in the early part with the first merger soon to happen

Fig.18 The standard design of Milton Bradley notes, first used in the **Game of Life** (MB, 1984) in 1960, and 3M notes from the games **Acquire** (1964) and **High Bid** (1965)

games with wide release there was a strong return to the simple race games of the nineteenth century, often sold on the basis of a gimmick – the game Ollman was trying to sell, *Class Struggle*, managed to be both overly complicated and a simplistic race at the same time, but with the marketing gimmick that it was designed as propaganda by a Marxist academic. Ollman was at the time denied a job in part largely for the political views expressed in the game[62]. At the same time a variety of smaller game publishers developed around much more complex games, aimed at small niche audiences. 3M and Sid Sackson's pursuit of more elegant mechanics and adult players brings us to another influential designer, Francis Tresham.

Capitalisation and Investment

> "Then leave Complaints: Fools only strive
> To make a Great an honest Hive.
> T' enjoy the World's Conveniencies,
> Befamed in War, yet live in Ease
> Without great Vices, is a vain
> Eutopia seated in the Brain.
> Fraud, Luxury, and Pride must live;
> Whilst we the Benefits receive."
>
> Mandeville, *The Fable of the Bees: Private Vice,*
> *Publick Benefits, 1714*

So far the types of stock market games discussed have been negative (punt games), or ambiguous (insider games), presentations of their subject. This is not a matter of selection but reflects that games representing the stock market tend to present it in negative terms or focusing on elements which are often perceived negatively. Even the earliest modern games, the *Bourse* games in chapter 1, were won by cornering markets, a serious breach of rules that would get you expelled from most exchanges.

However, in 1974, a designer called Francis Tresham, introduced two new innovations for the stock market game and the price track, and a much more positive depiction. The railway based *1829* has gone on to enduring success as a cult classic and spawned a series of successors known collectively as the *18XX* games. *1829* has two elements to the game: a map showing cities in nineteenth century England on which players mark out railway routes and run trains for different companies, and a stock market in which players buy and sell shares in those rail companies. The first innovation is in the price track, which is now arranged as a grid with each company marked by a counter, allowing more flexibility in movements than the fixed column predecessors. The second innovation is in what the shares do. When a player buys shares, the company they are buying them in gets capital which it can use to develop its network and trains. The successful development of the network is what drives the share price, so there is both a railway building game and a stock market game linked together.

What is interesting about this is the degree to which it reflects theoretical defences of the stock market. To understand these defences and how *1829* connects to them it is useful to draw an artificial distinction between investment and speculation. An investor buys a security directly from a company, with the promise of a share in the profit of the enterprise. In return the company is able to raise enough money for enterprises that a single person could not fund. In the seventeenth century joint stock arrangements like this were used to fund long distance trade, to India or the Americas, and in the nineteenth century they were used to generate the capital necessary to build railways. By contrast a speculator buys the security from some-one else and usually sells it again in a short space of time (this is known as a secondary market). The speculators money never reaches the company and their profit comes from price changes caused by expectation of the company's profit not from the actual results of the enterprise. Though investment and speculation have always been completely intertwined in the history of stock markets it will be unsurprising, given the games we have learnt about so far, that speculation was popularly understood to be a very negative activity.

> "Whate'er the wretched basely dare
> From Pride, Ambition, or Despair,
> Fraud, Luxury, or Dissipation,
> Assumes the Name of – SPECULATION"
>
> *Eighteenth Century Poem*[63]

Speculation was largely seen as gambling, or cheating, that served no useful purpose but only created unwanted effects on the market. The most dramatic of those effects were crashes in which speculation first raised prices of shares beyond any reasonable expectation of return and then dashed them, often causing hardship for those not directly involved. Crashes are as old as speculation. The South Sea Bubble of 1720 led to political debate and ultimately to the development of theoretical defences of speculation.

The defence mounted depended upon the degree to which speculation was essential to make investment possible. Early investors were committing their capital for long periods, often with no prospect of recovering any part of it for several years. This constrained the capital available for enterprises as investors would have to hold back sufficient funds to meet any unexpected expenses. If instead investors are able to dispose of their shares at any time they are more likely to invest, and speculators make excellent customers. A speculator can always find a price at which they will buy because there will always be a price at which they could realistically make a profit, or at least believe they could. As one economist observed on the worst days the New York exchange experience in 1929, not only were record numbers of shares sold but the same number were purchased.

One early pamphleteer put it like this:

> "It seems to be necessary, for the Support and Circulation of Publick Credit, that there should be a constant open Market, for the Sale and Purchase of the Funds, where every Person may have his Business transacted, for the Time, and in the Manner that suits him best, with Ease, Readiness, and Dispatch."[64]

It is worth noting the similarity between the defence of speculation and the defence of insider trading – not that the activity is moral but that it is useful.

The game *1829* incorporates this defence, quite possibly unintentional, alongside its emphasis on investment. Players are in no way incentivised to build railways at all. In the original rules Francis Tresham advised new players to focus on the stock market alone:

> "The recipe for novices competing against experts is simple; avoid directorships but otherwise get hold of as many shares as you can in the first three companies, plus any private companies that come your way, and HANG ONTO THEM – at least until you can see what is going on. Doing this, you will keep up with the experts surprisingly well. You can then try your hand at running one of the smaller railway companies – or settle down to quietly playing the stock exchange."[65]

1829 incentivises the players to behave as speculators, focusing on their own profits independent of the company's success. Yet despite this selfish behaviour the map ends up with a functional rail network for the United Kingdom – an advert to the players for the benefits of vice. This was the central argument in Mandeville's poem, The Fable of the Bees, which headed this section, that in economic activity individuals might cheat, be wasteful or unproductive, but that properly harnessed this behaviour can result in public benefit. *1829* embraces this in its simulation while largely glossing over the harms, such as poor health and safety, dislocations of people, and the speculation driven crash (known as the Railway Mania) which accompanied the early railways.

At first glance *1829* does not seem to have the makings of a successful game. The rules were complex enough Tresham felt the need to divide them into three parts, 'simple', 'intermediate', and 'full', to be learnt over several sessions – each of which would take well over three hours to play. There are no random elements so the game rewards careful study of its early positions, making it in many ways quite unsuited to family play. However, the *18XX* games found a steady audience amongst players interested in more complex games which flourished as the English-speaking market for family board games collapsed and the gaming market in general fragmented in the late 1970s and early 1980s (a topic for chapters 5 and 6). Perhaps some of *1829's* success is rooted in its positive portrayal of its subject, or maybe it was just a very good game. In any case this positive take on the stock market did not stick, and as the focus of family game design shifted from the UK to Germany in the 1980s the emphasis once more homed in on the negative consequences of speculation, this time with crashes.

Casino Capitalism and the Crashes

> "I literally remember walking down Wall Street on that Monday night and how you had this emotional image that you were walking through this Berlin 1945 landscape. It was very calm, very quiet. There was no sign of the turmoil that had gone on. It was a very frightening day."
>
> *Donald Donahue, financial regulator,*
> *reflecting on the 1987 Stock Market crash*[66]

Games like *1829* which paint an essentially positive picture of the stock market remain relatively rare. By the 1980s popular

Francis Tresham's Civilisation

Francis Tresham is equally famous for his game *Civilization*, published in 1980. Each player controls a vaguely defined great civilization (Babylonia, Egypt, Illyria, etc) and races to be the first to complete its journey through the Stone, Bronze, and Iron Ages. They do this by trading commodities (salt, grain, etc) to form sets with which various advances (pottery, metallurgy, philosophy) are purchased. Like *1829* it spawned its own sub-genre of games, known as 'Civ-games', and is widely regarded as a classic – despite requiring six or seven players and about five hours to play. The game does feature 'coinage' as a technology which permits the players to adjust levels of taxation – whether Tresham intended this as commentary on the historical role of coins or contemporary money is unclear.

interest in the financial world had reached a fever picture, as seen in popular films like Trading Places or Wall Street, and innovation in family board games was slowly shifting from the USA and UK to Germany. German designers would particularly focus on the crash.

A crash is a sudden and very large fall in the value of something, and it is often preceded by an unprecedented rise in value, known as a bubble. Bubbles and crashes can occur with anything that is bought and sold, for example in 1637 in Holland prices of tulips were subject to speculation involving a rapid rise and fall in prices known as the Tulip Mania. The existence of speculators anywhere securities or shares are sold, and particularly the ability of markets to create contracts (variously known as futures, time bargains, shorts, etc) on which a profit can be made by correctly predicting future prices, and potentially without owning the commodity, magnifies the risks of a crash. Famous examples include the South Sea Bubble of 1720, the Wall Street Crash of 1929, Black Monday in 1987, or the financial crisis of 2008, but in fact crashes have been a routine part of financial life since the eighteenth century. Which is not to say that nothing changed to bring the attention of German game designers to the subject. Some have argued that financial crashes have become more common in the 1980s and 90s, a formative period for German designers[67].

The phrase 'casino capitalism' was coined by the political scientist Susan Strange and evokes the risk of gambling, possibly reckless, in an arena it does not belong[68]. Strange believed a fundamental change in the nature of the financial world had taken place in the late twentieth century. Not only had the trades being made become detached from real-world activities, a complaint that had been around since the late seventeenth century, but Strange suggested that the system was increasingly opaque and the consequences of any crash were far greater than they had once been. Governments, regulators, and insiders, she claimed, no longer understood the system and its size and complexity had rendered it not only less stable but ensured that any shocks affect people entirely unrelated to the original speculation. This can be seen as an apt description of the financial crisis in 2008, which was precipitated by US banks making high risk loans. The loans were transformed into tradeable securities which not only prevented the danger from being seen but ensured that when people failed to pay them back it was often banks and investors on the other side of the world that suffered. Economists have criticised Strange's use of the term, suggesting it does not help us to understand the process (though that might miss some of the point that the process is fundamentally not understandable):

> "Casino capitalism was a potentially subversive way of de-
> scribing the most recent wave of market fundamentalism

in the UK and US, but it failed to realise its promise. Continuing to describe the current crisis in this way further abstracts international finance, making it less knowable and thus less accessible to criticism. The expression 'casino capitalism' makes disparate events and processes superficially familiar and similar in a way that obscures our efforts to understand them."[69]

We will focus on just one game inspired by the stock market and banking crashes of the late twentieth century. *Black Friday* was designed by Friedemann Friese and published in 2010. It is clearly a direct and very personal response to the crisis of 2008. Friese's first game, published in 1992 was *Wucherer* (literally 'profiteer'), republished in English as *Landlord*, and has obvious satirical overtones with players exploiting their tenants for a profit.

In *Black Friday* the price of various shares is recorded on a central price track in the same manner as in the *18XX* games. Whether the prices of stocks rise or fall is determined by drawing counters (shaped like brief-cases) from a bag, colour coded to the four groups of stock in the game. The players add counters, including black examples as they buy and sell. As the value of shares rise the number of black examples added increases and the players begin to draw more counters than they add. If enough black counters are drawn the shares fall in price.

Black Friday's shares are determined by a random mechanism, so they are not like those of *1829* which depend on the railway sub-game. Like the earlier punt games the share prices are divorced from the realities of making or selling things but the randomness works very differently to the dice-based movements of games like *Flutter*. In *Black Friday* if a share rises in one round because its counters are drawn it is less likely to rise in the next as there are now fewer counters in the bag (this is the difference between an independent and a dependent probability). As a result the shares always follow the same trajectory, they rise in value and then they fall (as the black counters are drawn later in the game). The players do affect this, if they buy more aggressively the price will rise more quickly and fall more dramatically afterwards, but this alters only the speed not the over-all trajectory.

Critically, both for the game-play and the satire, victory in *Black Friday* does not depend on holding the most cash at the end of the game (a marked difference with earlier stock market games). Instead players have the option of buying precious metals, the price of which rises over the course of the game. Gold and silver represent 'real' value, while stocks and paper money, appropriately marked with a capitalist vulture, possess only ephemeral worth.

*Fig.19 Paper money from **Black Friday** (Rio Grade, 2011) featuring a vulture as its central image*

The dynamic of crash game like *Black Friday* depends upon the reversal inherent in the game. At the beginning of the game the player only has very limited funds to buy precious metal, provided not from their own capital but in the form of public subsidies they will never be asked to pay back. Late in the game with share prices falling and precious metal rising the money will not go far, so victory goes to players who pick the right moment, buying shares in the rising market only to pull out just before the inevitable crash.

The game's simulation has very little to do with actual markets, as there are no derivative financial instruments of any of the types which played an important part in the crisis of 2008. The games model of how financial systems work, including the emphasis on buying and selling generic shares and its price track derive mostly from older board games, while elements such as the notion of 'real' value residing in precious metal owe more to popular discomfort with the changing nature of money than any deep analysis of the nature of stock market crashes. While its satirical elements are obvious it is unclear, as with *Ratrace* which was discussed earlier, whether that really matters. Do players engaging with *Black Friday* take away that crashes are destructive features of market systems resulting from poor regulation (the government subsidies) and reckless, immoral behaviour? Or, do they see financial success as a function of skill and crashes as inevitable cycles, which is what the victory conditions and mechanics imply?

Conclusion

> "… one can relish the varied idiocy of human action during a panic to the full, for while it is a time of great tragedy, nothing is being lost but money"
>
> *Kenneith Galbraith on the 1929 Crash*[70]

Designers, publishers, and players tend to be conservative, preferring to adapt and rework board games to produce slight variations rather than invent something entirely novel. As a result it is often possible to trace some common characteristics which link games together over a long period. In this chapter we have touched on a particular group of games themed around stock markets, all of which employ a similar price board as one of their central mechanics. These games have remained recognisably similar since they first appeared in the 1930s, but the ways in which they changed reflect important changes in popular understanding of financial institutions – at least for that section of society that designed, published, and played modern board games.

Broadly speaking the stock market games can be divided into four general classes which represent chronologically successive trends; the punt games that depicted speculation as gambling; the insider games which are clearly inspired by the controversial practice of insider trading; the brief dalliance with investor games in the 1970s; and finally, the focus on financial crashes when game design began to be dominated by German designers in the early 1990s. These phases of innovation and development are not just a story of game design but also a record of how money and finance were understood. An understanding which the games suggest focused on negative interpretations, features, or practices.

Why should this matter? For the study of games it gives a long-term thread that stretches over two periods of intense innovation (the commercialisation of modern board games in the 1930s and the development of the euro-game in the 1990s). This highlights prevailing design philosophies more clearly – the replacement of dice by cards in the switch from punt to insider games, or the features of the euro-games in the crash games. It also helps to clarify questions we might want to ask about games themselves; why, for example, have stock market games, with the notable exception of the *18XX* games, never enjoyed much commercial success? And for historians interested in broader questions there are the ways these games reflect broader social attitudes. Just one example will suffice. As suggested earlier, a recent trend in the study of nineteenth century financial institutions have suggested that insider trading of various sorts was rarely seen as immoral or inappropriate – and by implication that negative perceptions of it were a recent change in social attitudes. But is this really true? These studies largely depend on the records we have, and from the nineteenth century those mostly reflect the very insiders engaged in the practice – most of whom continued to see little wrong in insider trading long after it was heavily regulated and actively policed under public and political pressures. Games and their reception give us an alternative discourse, from people outside that world, people who might not otherwise articulate their opinion, or even consciously analyse the issue, but whose collective popular thinking on an issue is in many ways just as important. That is a set of voices that we can only really recover through this sort of evidence.

Lastly there is the vexed question of the impact games have. Does the negative framing of the stock market in games help to fuel negative public perceptions, or ultimately do people normalise the behaviours that bring victory? This is a topic we will return to in chapter 9.

It has been possible here only to touch lightly on the subject, but hopefully sufficiently to show the capacity of mundane objects to capture how money and finance are understood, and also to suggest their capacity to shape our understanding of those subjects[71].

4.
BOARD GAMES, *TOTOPOLY,*
AND THE ANTI-GAMBLING LEAGUE

"Gambling is a disease which spreads downwards to the industrious poor from the idle rich. In its most common form, betting on horse-racing, it is the only way in which the outcast plebeians can be joined with their betters in a bond of freemasonry. An elevating knowledge of distinguished jockeys and an exhilarating acquaintance with the pedigree of horses raise the poor parasite to the level of the rich one make them both men and brothers."

Ramsay MacDonald, British Politician, 1905[72]

Totopoly is not a particularly original game, but it is a rather unusual one, and its unusual elements reflect the odd history of gambling regulation, particularly horse racing, in the United Kingdom up to its publication in 1938. The game was designed by Walter Lee and Roy Vincent Palmer, two neighbours in the northern city of Leeds. It depicts the Lincoln Handicap, a horse race held since 1853 and one of the more important of the spring races in the English calendar. The twelve horses which appear are the winners of that race from 1926 to 1938.

Horse racing had been enjoyed by spectators for many centuries and 'gaming' (the wagering of money on the results) was a central part of the activity. However in the latter half of the nineteenth century improvements in communication and printing had made it possible to experience the thrill of gambling on horses vicariously. Bets could be placed with a local bookie based on the lists of entrants and the results printed in local newspapers. As a result betting became substantially more widespread, especially amongst the working class who had neither the spare time nor the income to attend races directly. And that made some people uncomfortable.

Many with strong religious convictions, or supporters of anti-gambling campaigns, opposed gambling generally, but some were specifically concerned with it as a class issue. The English middle class developed a coherent self-identity in the eighteenth and nineteenth century. A small part of that identity was wrapped up in appropriate notions of adult play – particularly card games such as *Whist*. When the middle class gambled on a hand of *Whist* it was a test of skill and they were moderate in their stakes – ideas expressed on whist counters made in the mid-nineteenth century. By contrast upper class gambling was reckless and extravagant, and working class gambling idle and liable to lead to ruin, financial or moral. Or at least that was how the middle class imagined it. The way people played united them and also marked social boundaries with those who played different sorts of games or in different locations. As Ramsay MacDonald (prime minister of the UK twice) hints at above when he associates the 'industrious poor' and 'idle rich'.

Fig.20 Anti-Gambling League Postcard from the first decade of the twentieth century

In the late nineteenth century concerns with a perceived increase in gambling led to the formation of the Anti-

Gambling League. Though much smaller than the temperance movement (which campaigned against alcohol) it had powerful friends such as the chocolate manufacturers Cadbury and Rowntree's (run by Quakers who had religious misgivings about gambling) which enabled it to mount effective political campaigns. Its biggest success was the passing of the 1906 Street Betting Act, which made it illegal to place cash bets anywhere other than at the venue of an event.

The effect was to immediately criminalise an important working class past-time. The wealthy upper classes who owned horses would obviously be at the track themselves, they could bet freely. Professional member of the middle class who enjoyed a flutter on the horses could continue to do so, as their banks would extend them credit and since that was not a cash transaction it was legal. The working class, who had neither opportunity to travel nor lines of credit, were directly targeted by the bill and they alone risked arrest. It was an inequity that was recognised even by anti-gambling campaigners, and would develop into a major political issue in the 1930s, though the law would not be repealed until 1960.

> "The state, we submit, should either prohibit betting altogether or recognise it. It should not direct its stings and arrows against the working man and refrain from interference from the rich man's gambling."
>
> *Alfred Cox (Secretary of the Society for the Suppression of Street Betting and Compulsory Registration)*[73]

And it was against this background, and based on the recently published *Monopoly*, that Walter Lee and Roy Palmer designed their game. They brought it to Waddingtons in late 1937, who agreed to publish it[74] and requested the designers file a patent. The game was published the following year and continued to be sold until 1943, when it likely stopped due to war time logistics. Publication resumed in 1950, when it caused a brief spat with Parker Brothers over the use of a name with the 'opoly' suffix[75]. It was eventually licensed to South Africa, India, Australia, and to Italy and France (under the misleading name *Ascot*), and is still in print today.

The board for *Totopoly* is two-sided and the game is played in two halves. Initially players are dealt cards representing both horses and various businesses. They must either pay the face value to acquire the cards or allow them to be auctioned (in which they can also bid). Then by rolling two dice horse proceed around the board track where players pay or receive money, and acquire 'advantage' and 'disadvantage' cards. Though this is no simple clone all of the individual elements derive from the *Landlord's Game* which Lee and Palmer must have played in the preceding year or two[76].

Once the first half is complete the board is turned over and players enter their horses into a race. Players place bets on which horse will win, and prizes are calculated for first, second, and third (based on the money spent on cards in the first half). The second half of the race then proceeds in a similar fashion to early twentieth century race games, each horse moving the distance indicated by a single die and any bonus or penalty for the space on which they land. A few interesting wrinkles are added, with a player gaining some control over the order in which they move their horses, it being possible to become blocked by other horses, and the outside and inside of the track differing in their effects. No individual part of the game is original but the over-all effect is to make *Totopoly* quite distinct from its contemporaries.

Several features are unusual. Firstly, quite distinct from almost any other horse racing game before or since it focuses on the whole process from training to race. Victor Watson commented specifically on this saying it is 'where it differs from every race game I have played'[77]. Subsequent horse racing games focusing almost exclusively on the race itself and the wagers. Palmer and Lee refer specifically to this aspect in their patents, intending the game to serve an educational purpose, to teach people about the whole sport.

The holistic approach likely reflected a sense that horse racing was misunderstood resulting from the contemporary political climate. In particular *Totopoly* is presenting very much an aspirational upper middle-class view of horse racing, in which the 'sport' is as much about training a horse as the race itself, both of which are to be experienced in person. In this sense the game is an idealised version of a particular group's experience of horse racing, in many ways detached from most peoples' experience. This probably also explains one odd rule anomaly found in early versions – that the winner of the game would be the player whose horse finished first in the race. The rule is at odds with the structure of the game and its inspirations, which would suggest the winner ought to be the player with the most money. A similar rule was included in a slightly later football game, *Wembley*, where the winner is not the player who best manages their teams to achieve a profit but the owner of the team that wins the competition. It is possible that someone felt uncomfortable with a focus on the financial aspect, preferring that the game be played for the spectacle of the race. Whether this was the designers or the publisher is unclear.

The second interesting feature of *Totopoly* is the complexity of the rules and the elaborate nature of the production. In 1938 there simply was no other board game on the market remotely as complex as *Totopoly*. Player's functionally had to learn two distinct games, both using familiar mechanics but mixed in unusual ways or with novel modifications. And the game itself had a lot in it, painted metal horses, tickets for the races, several

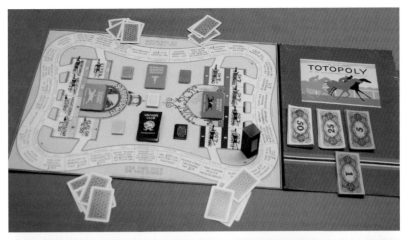

*Fig.21 The **Totopoly** (Waddingtons, 1938) board is two-sided, each dedicated to two halves of the game, the first based on **Monopoly**, the second based on older race games*

different decks of cards, and the elaborate double-sided three-fold board. The game very much required adult players, even if it could accommodate younger members of a family, and it seems unlikely Waddington's would have taken such a chance if not for the recent success of board games like *Monopoly*[79].

House Rules

No less an authority than the games designer Francis Tresham once remarked that *Totopoly* was a good game if you ignored the rules[78]. He was referring, with some characteristic hyperbole, to declaring the player with the most money the winner. It is common for regular players to modify rules for a variety of reasons, and often with variable success, usually known as 'house rules'.

There are various common house rules used with *Totopoly*. The most common, already mentioned, is to declare the winner to be the player with the most money – which seems to better fit the spirit of the rules (at least to someone not living through the controversial regulation of gambling in 1938).

Another house rule is to extend the auction at the start of the game. The face value of the cards is generally lower than their actual value to players encouraging them to be purchased outright rather than auctioned, and giving those with a fortunate deal an advantage. If each player is dealt only one card (including the auctioneer card) the game takes longer but involves more skill.

Some players also make the betting on the horse race secret, and sometimes seed the pot by placing a bet made up of the entry fees. This is done because good players otherwise make very strange bets. It is clear that Watson and Palmer simply assumed players would bet as they would on an actual horse race and never considered that the constraints of a game might create different incentives.

"Our first glimmer of interest in racing came from playing the new dice game Totopoly. We found it more thrilling than Monopoly, and I can remember the best horses, Dark Warrior and Dorigen, haunting my dreams."

Lord Acton[80]

Totopoly saw gradually increasing sales after the Second World War (when the young Lord Acton first played it) and slowly established itself as an important part of Waddington's line. The game was not as important as to Waddington as *Cluedo*, and not as innovative as the later racing game, *Formula 1*, but is still fondly by nostalgic players.[81] However, in a sign of the changing nature of the toy industry the company stopped paying royalties to the designers and their families in 1968[82]. The company claimed that it only owed royalties for the lifetime of the patent, which had expired some years before, though that was not Roy Palmer's understanding and the original agreement, preserved in the archives of the company, is hard to read in that way.[83] Likely the decision was motivated by rising sales, and thus an increase in royalty payments. The board games business was becoming a less cosy affair, Waddington's relationship with Parker Brothers which had once depended on a friendly correspondence encompassing contemporary politics and family holidays had been replaced with formal contracts reached through hard negotiation.[84] Companies were increasingly focusing on the bottom line – maximizing the profit for each game and seeking out those which reached the widest possible audiences. Where this more business-like approach took board games, will be the subject of the next chapter.

5.
WHY *OPERATION* HAS MONEY
AND OTHER QUESTIONS ABOUT
THE DEATH OF BOARD GAMES...

"It's called Christmas. You know, the time when people walk
around with those boxes marked 'How to Be Taken for A
Complete Sucker', and of which we are reliably informed
50% are never opened, let alone played."

Brian Walker, Games Journalist, 1987[85]

The transformation of modern board games, from the hobby
of a few American enthusiasts to millions of commercial copies
worldwide in the 1930s was followed by a period of innovation
and expansion. The resulting games were often well-suited to
play by families, engaging and challenging enough for the adults,
but simple enough in terms of rules to be followed by children,
and the term 'family game' would be a reasonable substitute for
'modern'. However, the market was to collapse in the 1980s.

Already by the 1970s a definite malaise was apparent, and modern
board games were once more becoming the hobby of a handful
of enthusiasts. A few modern games had 'stuck', particularly
Monopoly, Cluedo, Risk, and *Scrabble.* The last had even achieved
the transition to a hobby in its own right like *Chess,* but finding
other games, especially by the 1980s, at least in the English-
speaking world, would require resorting to specialist stores or
mail order. Toy companies did continue to publish new games,
especially in the run up to Christmas when the bulk of sales
occurred, but many of them had reverted to pre-1930 design
philosophies, such as the 1974 game *Follyfoot.*

Follyfoot has the overt trappings of a modern board game. Players
are each given an initial supply of money and as they traverse
the outer circuit of the board they gain or lose it. Once they

have completed one or two circuits they enter their horse into the gymkhana event depicted at the centre of the board, and win prize money depending on where they place. The similarity of that description to *Totopoly* (chapter 4) is probably not coincidental.

However, this is deceptive. In terms of its mechanics *Follyfoot* is actually a traditional race game of a slightly unusual type, in which players receive or surrender tokens when they land on spaces rather than being moved forwards or backwards. The game is then won by the player with the most tokens at the end. This format of traditional race games lends itself to gambling and that probably explains why in nineteenth century Britain and America it was rarer than those in which the first player to the end wins. Both types share the same dynamic, the winner is decided solely by chance with skill playing no part, but they achieve it through different mechanics.

Follyfoot was based on a television series that ran from 1971 and which was primarily aimed at teenagers rather than young children[86]. It is unclear if they would have been satisfied by a slightly more complex versions of the games marketed at very young children, certainly the games journalist Brian Walker, quoted above, thought they would be disappointed.

Historians have not offered an adequate answer to why the market for family games collapsed. Likely there was no single cause but a complex set of factors, some of which are fairly obvious. Board games had to compete with new forms of entertainment, particularly television and video games. The latter posed a fairly direct threat and it was seen as inevitable in some quarters that computers would eventually obsolete their manual predecessors. In the United Kingdom, which some players considered an important centre for innovation,[87] the toy industry in general suffered a catastrophic financial collapse resulting both from a general economic downturn and industry specific issues. Most board games manufacturers are also toy manufacturers and this naturally had a large knock on effect. In the United States there was a pronounced shift to large chains of toy shops and television advertising which raised the bar for entry into the toy market, encouraging manufacturers to focus on games which would reach the largest possible audiences, or which were already well known.

Games manufacturers had never stopped making traditional games, either the simple race games aimed at children or the abstract strategy games like *Chess* aimed primarily at adults. It was relatively easy to take popular subjects and adapt them to simple race games, as in the case of *Follyfoot*, certainly much easier than developing or adapting novel mechanics. Even for a critical eye it would be relatively hard to establish if such a game was a modern family game in the style of *Totopoly* (see chapter 2) or *Acquire* (see chapter 3), without actually playing it, and most games were bought, as Brian Walker suggests, at Christmas, by people other than those who would play them.

Games as Toys

"This is not a game, this is nothing. A game, you play it on a board and you roll dice but this, this is a lot of plastic junk. We can't use this."

Reputedly the response of the Milton Bradley company to Mouse Trap[88]

The family board game also acquired a new competitor in 1963 with the release of *Mouse Trap*, and just two years later by *Operation*. Both games were developed by Marvin Glass, the latter based on a design by John Spinello. Marvin Glass' company did not make toys, it developed ideas which it then sold to toy companies. And in the mid-1960s it struck on the idea of making its children's toys, especially those involving dexterity, look like games.

John Spinello was a student at the University of Illinois when he developed a toy in which players tried to navigate a metal probe along a groove. He later showed it to a model maker at Marvin Glass and Associates who was sufficiently impressed to take it to the head of the company. They purchased the rights from him and subsequently brought it to games company Milton Bradly, who were keen not to miss out a second time having previously rejected *Mouse Trap*. It was there that the idea of removing objects and the medical theme were added.

Operation has become one of the most successful toys of the mid-1960s but it really has no more in common with modern board games than they do with traditional games like *Chess* or the children's race games of the nineteenth century. It is a genuinely clever dexterity puzzle given the trappings of a contemporary board game by the addition of paper money (in denominations of 50 and 200 in the original game and 100 and 500 in most recent licensed variants). If you played *Operation* as a child and think there may not have been money in your version you are in good company. While writing this book I had conversations about *Operation* with many people and almost no-one remembered the money, some were certain it was absent in their copy (with in one case opening the box demonstrating the contrary).

Why is the money in *Operation* so forgettable? The answer is because it is entirely redundant, at least for the purposes of the game. Each small plastic piece that must be removed from 'Cavity Sam' without causing his nose to buzz is assigned a cash value by the cards, but this money is not subsequently used to buy anything, it is simply a points tally. The game could have framed this simply as points, and they could have been easily tracked on a score pad, or simply by retaining and adding up the cards at the end of the game. And as *Operation* is an enjoyable and challenging puzzle or toy without any of the structure provided by rules or victory conditions you could easily discard the money, or simply leave it under Cavity Sam's tray undisturbed – which it seems many players did. Of course, what the use of Milton Bradley's standard note did was to connect *Operation* more concretely to the rest of its line of games, such as *Game of Life* (1960), *Go for Broke* (1960), and *Smuggle*[89]. *Operation* has paper money because it wanted to look like a game and in 1965 nothing looks more like a game than paper money.

The Dark Days

> "[The] gamer's paradise at that time was Great Britain. We used to pilgrimage to London once or twice a year to buy games. The reason for this prosperous production was a very intense market communication with high credibility. Information was provided not only by the manufacturers but above all by competent game critics who published their reviews in major newspapers."
>
> *Tom Werneck*[90]

Werneck is reflecting with these words on the early 1970s, when board games had become sufficiently popular to make magazines dedicated to them, such as the short lived 'Games and Puzzles' (1972-1981) seem like a good idea.

The tendency today, under the influence of all-encompassing community web forums like BOARD GAME GEEK, is to think of all board games as belong to a single coherent hobby. This makes a lot of sense as it is extremely difficult to offer concrete definitions for what distinguishes a card game, a dexterity game, a family, adult, strategy, or abstract game, without accepting at least the possibility of a lot of vague exceptions at the edges. That elides a great deal of internal difference though, the people who routinely play *Bridge* are not the same as those who play *Chess* or *Scrabble*, and enthusiasts for contemporary games would not play *Snakes & Ladders*. As an anecdotal illustration of this I own a t-shirt which displays the names of recent game designers (the oldest being Sid Sackson and most being post-1990) as a word-cloud. I once met a collector of post-war family board games who was very knowledgeable but did not recognise a single name.

Historical definitions are easier to draw than general ones, because only certain games were published and only a relatively modest number of those were successful, and at specific moments in time they tend to have things in common. A useful distinction is made by Stewart Woods, in his book Eurogames, between 'mass-market' and 'hobby' games which encapsulates the situation that arose from the late 1970s to the early 1990s. In that period where a game was sold (in major stores or small specialist shops) would give you clues as to its contents. Some companies tried to bridge that gap, for example Milton Bradley attempted to bring wargames to the mass market in the early 1980s and role-playing games in 1991.

In general toy industry insiders in this period were increasingly out of touch with people who actually played board games. They were convinced that, as with toys in general, only television advertising could sell new products[91], though the most successful phenomena in the period, role-playing games (chapter 6), fantasy miniature wargames like Games Workshop, collectible card-games, and the euro-games (chapter 7), all succeeded largely on word of mouth. At the same time hobby games had adapted to their small niche audiences, often producing elaborately complex products that require substantial investments of time and money. Neither really made for good family games.

This has led to a legacy in terms of the understanding people have of board games. There has been a lively production of modern board game suitable for family audiences since the

Fig.22 Banknotes from the game Operation using the post-1960 Milton Bradley design, the transitional, and the post-1996 Hasbro design

1990s, driven by a German market that was forced to innovate when it could no longer import. Yet players of those games often do not recognise the connection between what they play and the innovations in modern board games from the 1930s to 1960s, precisely because of this period of fragmentation in the 1970s and 80s. A quote from Stewart Woods describing mass-market games will illustrate this:

> "... *Scrabble, Monopoly ... The Game of Life ... Clue ... Candyland* ... have continued to sell well long after their initial publication. Over time the rules to these games have become a part of the Western cultural lexicon and are easily transferred from one generation to the next. A result of this is that the shelves of large retail outlets are typically dominated by games that were, in many cases,

designed more than half a century ago. While these games might be termed 'classic' in the sense that they occupy a central position in the cultural understandings of board and table games, they have arguably, acquired this status largely through a combination of manufactured nostalgia and effective marketing"[92]

Hopefully chapter 2 made the case that *Monopoly* owes its place in board games history to more than manufactured nostalgia, and a game as successful as *Scrabble* surely needs no defence[93]. Their juxtaposition with *Candyland*, a simple race game, indicates the extent to which many games which survived the fragmentation of the 1980s as commercial successes have been tainted by association – at least in the eyes of those who would describe themselves as hobby gamers.

Conclusion

"There are in America today individuals and companies who do nothing but apply their ingenuity to the construction and invention of games with which to amuse the public and thereby derive their sustenance. Yet despite this concentration of effort, the dice-and-board games of today do not differ in principle from those of the Aztecs and the Hindus."

Charles John Erasmus, Anthropologist, 1950[94]

We saw in chapter 2 how those historians and anthropologists who first developed the study of board games as a serious academic endeavour failed to recognise, or in some cases even acknowledge the existence, of modern board games. They viewed, as Erasmus does, the new games as a simple continuity with ancient race games enlivened only a little by advances in printing technology since the seventeenth century. As demonstrated in that chapter they were spectacularly wrong in their assessment, but they could not have been so far of the mark without a reason.

Modern board games have only ever been a relatively small part of board games in general. More readers of this book will have played a traditional race game like *Snakes & Ladders*, than will have played even very successful modern games like *Monopoly*, *Acquire*, or *Settlers of Catan*. Likewise for traditional games with no random element; *Noughts & Crosses*, *Chess*, and *Go* undoubtedly remain more widely played than any single modern game, excepting possibly *Scrabble*. Traditional card games are probably even more widely played. And this has been the case since modern board games first enjoyed commercial success in the 1930s.

So the type of game being discussed already represents a niche within its own category, and also a niche with the toy industry. Simple race games continued to dominate the market for children's games[95], and traditional card or abstract games the market for older players, even while designers of modern games innovated new mechanics for several decades. It is not hard to see how academic observers, who were probably not players of the modern games, could miss their significance, hidden as they were from an outsider amongst so much continuity with the past.

Fig.23 Industrial Production Certificate from the game Axis & Allies (Avalon Hill, 2004) Milton Bradley produced the second edition as part of an attempt to develop mass-market versions of hobby games. The wargames they chose frequently focused on the economic aspect of warfare.

At the same time this might explain the commercial vulnerability of such games. Faced with competition from new types of games – role-playing and wargames for older players, toy-like games such as *Operation* for younger ones, video games for all ages – it was easy for them to be squeezed from the market in the late 1970s and early 1980s. Other explanations for the demise of these games might include the increasing domination of the industry by a few very large toy companies uninterested in innovation; wider changes in the entertainment industry; or more pronounced social changes among the family audiences who would once have played the games on an evening.

Whatever the cause the consequences were clear. The period of innovation which had begun with commercial success of *Landlord's Game* variants in the 1930s and had led to a host of radically new games, some financial others not, into the 1960s, largely came to an abrupt end. It became increasingly difficult to find more than a handful of the most popular modern games in high-street stores, and innovative or original designs produced by major companies largely ceased, with the exception of a few titles trying to find mass-appeal options for trends in wargames or role-playing games.

In Germany, however, there was a continued demand for family board games (suitable for children but interesting for adults) continued. As the 1980s proceeded the demand in Germany for such games, which had previously depended on UK and US imports, would lead to new innovation locally and a marked evolution of the modern board game, often referred to as 'eurogames', which will be examined in chapters 7 and 8.

6.
IMAGINING SMAUG'S TREASURES

"Beneath him, under all his limbs and his huge coiled tail, and about him on all sides stretching away across the unseen floors, lay countless piles of precious things, gold wrought and unwrought, gems and jewels, and silver red-stained in the ruddy light.

Smaug lay with wings folded like an immeasurable bat, turned partly on one side, so that the hobbit could see his underparts and his long pale belly crusted with gems and fragments of gold from his long lying on his costly bed. Behind him where the walls were nearest could be dimly seen coats of mail, helms and axes, swords and spears hanging; and there in rows stood great jars and vessels filled with a wealth that could not be guessed."

J.R.R Tolkien, The Hobbit

Tolkien scholars have long recognised that greed is a central motif in his novels, for material wealth in *The Hobbit* (1937) and for power in *The Lord of the Rings* (1954-5)[96]. It seems reasonable to assume, as a group of economists did in late 2012, that Smaug, the dragon whose treasure Bilbo sets out to steal, sits atop a hoard of precious metal coins, of money. In a series of blog posts they wondered whether Thrain's greed was really sound financial policy, if Smaug's hoarding might have been deflationary, and what role a post dragon-slaying boom might have had in the rise to power of the dark lord Sauron[97]. All of which depended on the assumption that Smaug's hoard was composed of gold 'specie' (coins intended for general circulation at a value based on their metal content). These ideas are particularly reasonable since when Bilbo is first hired for the job he is specifically offered one-fourteenth, after expenses, 'in cash'. Yet in the lengthy description of the dragon's hoard Tolkien never mentions coins or even the more abstract 'money'.

In Tolkien's narratives the presence or absence of money plays an important role. Money is extensively referred to at the beginning of each novel, in Bilbo's homeland of the Shire, and also serves an important role in resolving problems once characters return home, such as the auction of Bilbo's belongings after he is presumed dead during his long absence.[98] In between money is rarely mentioned, even in scenes such as the description of Smaug's hoard where it would be entirely logical for it to feature.

That Tolkien is using money to draw a sharp distinction between the mundane world, represented by the Shire, and the heroic world in which the adventures take place is clear from two episodes.[99] In *The Hobbit* the first adventure Bilbo has is with three trolls; it begins with him attempting to steal a purse and ends with the discovery of a pot of gold coins which the characters bury. This is the only reference to coins. It is paralleled by a scene in the *Lord of the Rings*, where upon arriving at the village of Bree the party's mules are stolen and must be replaced. Exclusively at this moment Tolkien breaks the flow of the narrative to give a detailed accounting of the price of mules and thirty silver pennies that change hands.

> "Bill Fenny's price was twelve silver pennies; and it was indeed at least three times the pony's value in those parts. It proved to be a bony underfed, and dispirited animal; but it did not look like dying just yet. Mr Butterbur paid for it himself, and offered Merry another eighteen pence as some compensation for the lost animals"
>
> *(Lord of the Rings: A Knife in the Dark)*

This use of money to reinforce the difference between mundane and heroic world reflects a similar distinction in the folk and epic literature Tolkien was imitating. That it was deliberate is testified to by changes from the early drafts. In *The Hobbit* chapter, A Conversation with Smaug, when Bilbo is needled by the dragon Tolkien first had him respond 'that money was no object or only a secondary one' but soon corrected his manuscript with the line which finally appeared 'that gold was only an afterthought'[100]. Likewise in preparing notes for what would eventually become Appendix F on The Languages and Peoples of the Third Age Tolkien wrote an aside on the word

Fig.24 Metallic coins (Ulfsark, 2015) produced as props for games, representing dwarven money and in part based on images created by Tolkien.

for quarter 'in Gondor *tharni* was used for a silver coin, the fourth part of the *castar* (in Noldorin the *canath* or fourth part of the *mirian*)'[101] which would have confirmed the use of coined money amongst both men and elves if it had not been excised from the published version[102].

When *The Hobbit* was adapted into a series of films between 2012 and 2014 much of this was changed. Bilbo does not attempt to steal a purse from the trolls but a knife, and though coins are scattered on the cave floor it is a chest of jewellery and goblets the dwarves bury. On the other hand Smaug's treasure is clearly an immense mound of coins[103]. So how did we get from money as a symbol of the mundane world to the principle goal of the adventure? The answer is almost certainly *Dungeons & Dragons*.

Dungeons & Dragons and Role-Playing Games

"Once you get into it you will never be the same"

Advert for the game Hero Quest, 1991[104]

Dungeons & Dragons, or simply *D&D*, was initially developed by Gary Gygax and Dave Arneson as a small-scale wargame, expanding on an earlier set of rules, *Chainmail*, and first published in 1974. It would soon outgrow its origins as a wargame and with its many successors develop into the new hobby of roleplaying. In roleplaying games (RPG) players control a single character who inhabits a fictional world, a fantasy world drawing heavily on authors like Tolkien in the case of *D&D*. One player, the game master, is responsible for describing the world the characters inhabit and resolving the adventures they undertake. The games master is neither an opponent nor a player, but rather a sort of umpire who adjudicates the results of the character's actions. RPGs, and in particular *D&D*, allow the players to imagine a complex and complete world, one in which money plays a central part.

From 1977 to 2000 *D&D* was produced in two different versions, usually referred to as 'basic' and 'advanced', which both had various editions. Though at least seven sets of rules can be clearly distinguished, they all use the same monetary system and the acquisition of money is a central part of the game. The core of D&D's money is a trimetallic decimal system, in which gold coins are the standard unit and are worth ten silver coins and one hundred copper coins[105].

Until very recently most coins were indeed made from precious metals, with gold, silver, and various copper alloys being common choices. That element of D&D's economy makes sense (though systems of credit, banknotes and transferable financial instruments are older than is often assumed). However, in pre-thirteenth century Europe, which is the reference point for both Middle Earth and *D&D* the standard unit was a silver penny, not a gold coin, and it was usually the only coin in circulation. Tolkien, as one would expect of a medieval scholar gets this right in his description of silver pennies in Bree. True trimetallic systems do not work very well because fluctuations in the relative value of the metals disrupt them. The Roman Empire did for a period in the first centuries BC and AD maintain such a system but it depended on silver and copper coins being substantially over-valued and was far from stable. In other ancient states where coins were made in different metals, such as the Sasanian Empire in Iran (third to seventh century AD), the coins were used for very different purposes; silver as the standard of exchange, gold for reasons of royal patronage usually issued only in association with coronations; and copper for local civic uses.

However, D&D's system is not based on ancient examples but the projection of modern concepts (including the decimal system). To a group of young Americans in the early 1970s it would be logical for gold to be the standard unit. The 'gold standard' as a backing for circulating currency dominated twentieth century discussions of economics. The United States had suspended the convertibility of gold in 1971, and in 1974 permitted private ownership of gold, important elements in ending that standard but also events the designers would have known about simply from reading a newspaper.

Likewise the ubiquity of money in *D&D* is a modern convention. Consider how often characters in Tolkien's world depend upon hospitality or gifts – a feature of the kind of epic literature written in societies that were not heavily monetised on which he drew. Yet in *D&D* money is everywhere, with any group of travellers (human, elven, orc, or goblin) likely to be carrying coins, but it also plays a central role as a standard. Take for example the 'basic' rules first published in 1983, one of the most widely played editions of the game. The cover of the first rule book is adorned with a red dragon on a heap of treasure, perhaps loosely inspired by Tolkien's depiction of Smaug. In that version gold pieces are the standard monetary unit, they are also the standard unit of weight, and earning a gold piece earns the character one point of experience (which are used to gain levels and improve the characters abilities).

If Smaug was a red dragon (dragons in *D&D* are colour-coded) in that version then his defeat would earn the characters 2300 experience points. However, he would also be sitting on hoard that would contain some gems, some magical items, and about 80,000 coins. It would take a substantial team of pack mules to move such a treasure, a problem Tolkien has Bilbo and his dwarven companions ponder at some length. In this version of *D&D* liberating the dragon of that treasure would grant the players approximately 47,000 experience points, far more than they would receive for the dirty business of killing him, which neither Bilbo nor the dwarves do. Where Tolkien eliminated money to mark the transition into the heroic world, D&D projects a modern ubiquitous monetary system into the heart of its fantasy, something that has been avidly embraced by its players ever since.

So what? Well I would suggest that this matters because *D&D* both reflects and informs wider understandings of pre-modern money. It is probably more important than any book written by a numismatist in shaping popular understanding of pre-modern money. Games inspired by *D&D* use a gold standard. The board game *Heroquest,* published by mainstream games company Milton Bradley in 1991 (with the TV advertising and mainstream distribution that entailed) but actually designed by

Fig.25 Heroquest provided an opportunity for main-stream audiences to experience elements of role-playing games like Dungeons & Dragons. In this mission players must enter the dungeon and recover stolen gold.

fantasy wargame manufacturer Games Workshop, uses gold as its currency. The online computer game, *World of Warcraft*, uses a trimetallic decimal system with a standard gold unit[106]. No small matter since the virtual economy of *World of Warcraft* is larger than many national economies[107].

But the impact is not limited to games which are derivative of D&D. When the license to make a role-playing game based on Middle Earth was granted in 1984 that game featured a tri-metallic monetary system rather than one derived from Tolkien's own work. When Forbes magazine created a list of the wealthiest fictional characters *D&D* was used as a definitive reference for Smaug's size[108]. In George R R Martin's popular series of fantasy novels, *A Song of Ice and Fire*, though he draws heavily on actual medieval history for many elements (particularly the War of the Roses) his monetary economy is a trimetallic system obviously indebted to *D&D*.

7.
CLEVER HANS AND THE EURO-GAMES

'The Germans have a wonderful knack of marrying abstract problems with perfect themes...'[109]

Review in Games International, 1988

The Spiel de Jahre (Game of the Year), an annual award for board games, began in 1979. Though it is often assumed Germany had a long tradition of modern board games, just as it has a long tradition of toy manufacture, in fact at the time it was mostly dependent on foreign innovation. The Spiel de Jahre is restricted to games published in Germany and today is usually awarded for games published in that year, but in 1979 it was given to a German reprint of *Hare and Tortoise*, actually first published in 1973 by an English designer. In 1980 it went to *Rummikub*, developed in Israel, and in 1981 for *Focus*, by the American designer Sid Sackson, both originally published many years earlier. When German games did win, such as *Scotland Yard* in 1983 (a deduction game in which detectives chase the villainous Mr.X around London), the game was obviously published with an English-speaking audience in mind (the original German board is printed with English labels) and the vaunted Spiel de Jahre logo was omitted in editions sold outside of Germany.

Though German board games had been highly derivative of the American and English markets since the 1950s, this would change in the 1980s. In 1982 when an annual games fair was established in Essen it attracted just 2000 attendees. By 1988 Essen was attracting 65,000 people, and the Spiel de Jahre was hugely boosting sales of the winning game in Germany[110]. English-speaking games journalists were not only beginning to notice German games but to attribute to them a distinct design philosophy.

The production of modern board games aimed at a family audience expanded in Germany, developing its own distinctive trends, largely in response to the disappearance of such games in the UK and USA. This led to the success of new manufacturers, such as Hans im Glück (named for a fairy tale 'clever Hans' or 'Hans in luck'), who published original games exclusively in German with no attempt to market their games internationally. This isolation of the German game industry, for nearly a decade, ensured that when it was noticed abroad in the 1990s the games appeared both fresh and innovative.

Fig.26 Mr. X leaves the British Museum, but can he escape. A German edition of the game **Scotland Yard** *(Ravensburger, 1984)*

The broad outlines of this historical shift are clear but a lot of questions remain. Why, for example, did this sort of modern family game persist in Germany when they were so effectively displaced by other factors (such as industry change, gamified toys, video games, role-playing and wargames) in the English-speaking world? And why, since some players continued to keep up with trends in Germany did it take until the mid-1990s for the games to enjoy enough success to warrant English-language editions? The latter is a particularly important question as it was the isolation which made them distinctive enough to deserve a name of their own, the euro-games.

Early Reactions – the Grognards

> "This version was very popular in Europe and won KREMLIN "Game of the Year" accolades in Germany. However, it was met with disdain by our veteran stateside playtesters and I personally much prefer our version."
>
> *David Greenwood on the game Kremlin* [111]

The term 'grognard' was coined by John Young in the 1970s in reference to the soldiers of Napoleon's old guard and popularised by the wargames magazine *Strategy & Tactics*. Grognard refers to a player whose taste in games tends towards older games often with a grumpy dismissal of the new. A flavour of this is apparent in the translation of the game *Kremlin* to the American market. Avalon Hill's David Greenwood was tasked to adapt *Kremlin* for a US audience long before German games became fashionable, and his first action was to relegate the original victory conditions to an optional rule.

The final Avalon Hill version also contained a set of 'advanced rules'. Usually advanced rules are understood to be the correct rules for the game and basic rules are used simply as training exercises in order to make complex games digestible. Greenwood's remarks above show that the original game was not seen as simple but as simplistic, though it is noteworthy that there was some opposition to these changes as he goes on to record:

> "Alan Moon, a recent comrade-in-arms, differs with me in this respect. He feels that the chance cards bastardise the pure strategy aspect of the game. For my part, I feel that they increase the opportunities to formulate a strategy and, more importantly, introduced hilarious opportunities for sudden twists of fate."

Alan Moon would go on to design one of the examplars of the euro-game, *Ticket to Ride*, which won the Spiel de Jahre in 2004. He was an early proponent of the design philosophy developed in Germany and also a playtester for one of my personal favourite games, *Civilization*. *Civilization* was originally designed and published by Francis Tresham (see chapter 3) in 1980. Like *Kremlin* it was also redesigned by Avalon Hill's playtesters in the late 80s and I have always had a very similar visceral dislike of that version which seems to reject much of the simplicity and elegance of the original.

Defining the Euro-Game

> '... how we do use the word "game". For how is the concept of a game bounded? What still counts as a game, and what no longer does? Can you say where the boundaries are? No. You can draw some, for there aren't any drawn yet. (But this never bothered you before when you used the word "game".)'
>
> *Ludwig Wittgenstein, Philosopher, 1953*[112]

Before going any further a short definition of 'euro-game' is in order. This is difficult because defining the term 'game' itself is

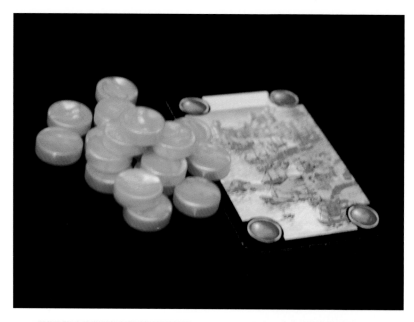

Fig.27 A card from the euro-game Bohnanza (Amigo, 1997) depicting a gold coin on the reverse, and a pile of gold tokens from the game Citadels (Hans im Glück, 2000)

hard. In fact in philosophy 'game' is frequently used to illustrate the difficulty of definition[113]. It gets a little easier if contemporary usage is ignored and we instead focus on those games which enjoyed critical success in the late 1990s and early 2000s[114]. Even so, not all games made in Germany were euro-games partly because the category depends both on design philosophy and critical reception – in other words German manufactures just thought they were making games, it was only when English language players began selectively importing them that the concept of the euro-game developed.

In terms of game mechanics there are three important features of euro-games. First, the games tend to be relatively short, often under an hour, and also much more predictable in their length than both older games and UK and US hobby games of the same period. For example in *Modern Art*, one of the earliest euro-games published in 1992, there are a fixed number of rounds after which the winner is the player with the most money, contrasting with the earlier game *High Bid* in which the game ends when one player achieves a certain net worth. Secondly, the designs favoured restricting player's actions. In the game *Money!* each player makes exactly one purchase on their turn, regardless of how much they spend. Euro-games also tended to favour certain types of mechanics, such as auctions, set-collection, and majority control. Finally, and probably the most important and distinctive feature was that euro-games used dependent probability. That is the chance of something happening is affected by what has already happened, something usually associated with cards or tiles rather than dice (which usually involve independent probabilities) [115]. The preference for dependent probability, and rejection of dice, was such a marked feature that though between 1979 and 1995 nine games featuring dice won the Spiel de Jahre, not a single winning game used dice from 1996 until *Camel Up* won in 2014[116].

There are also elements of theme and play dynamic which if not distinctive at least represented strong trends. Euro-games very rarely focus on warfare or conflict, but do have a preference for building, especially with historic themes focusing on medieval or early modern European history, which will be explored in the next chapter on *Alhambra*. They tend not to give players the option to directly harming another player, preferring more indirect competitions. As a result euro-games feel more like a race and less like a conflict.

There are also aesthetic elements which made euro-games stand out. The designer's name tends to appear on the cover, a feature which had not been seen since the 1930s. For this reason 'designer game' is often used as synonym for euro-game. The boxes tend to be a different size, deep squares rather than shallow rectangles, and the pieces tended to be wooden rather than plastic, as low print runs favoured small set-up costs over savings of scale. Lastly, and often over-looked, is the widespread replacement of paper money with representations of coins. This last aesthetic change reflects changing perceptions of value and will be the focus of the rest of this chapter.

Why do Euro-Games Have Coins?

"The money, however, is a terrible waste of paper. It is done in the style of *Monopoly* money, only smaller. Since you are constantly changing in money, they get folded, torn, etc. Personally, I recommend poker chips. It's easier to see how much money you have and (more importantly) how much your opponent has. The paper money is just plain sad."

Online review of Power Grid by Joshua Noa [117]

It is important to consider both insider and outsider perspectives of modern games in order to get a complete picture of the phenomenon. While these views are often incompatible and neither is entirely 'true', they can complement each other, helping to give a strong insight into social phenomenon the games represent.

Let us begin with the insider understanding of the absence of paper money in euro-games, how people who play games explain it. Fortunately, the game *Power Grid* helps us understand the view of at least those English-speaking gamers who regularly post on community websites. *Power Grid* was designed by Friedemann Friese as *Funkenschlag* and published in 2001, before being revised for an international audience in 2004. The board is a map of Germany showing major cities and connections between them. Players use money to establish a network between the cities, to purchase power plants and to buy fuel to run the power plants. Competition is relatively indirect; connecting a city before another player costs less, as does buying fuel, and power plants are distributed by auction (a favoured euro-game mechanic) but in such a way that every player gets one. At the end of each round the players use fuel to activate power plants which run cities, and based on the number of cities they run they receive cash. It is one of the most critically acclaimed games of the euro-game period, but unlike most of its contemporaries *Power Grid* uses paper money.

The paper money in *Powergrid* receives a lot of comments in reviews and on forums. This is usually framed in terms of ergonomics – paper money is bad at its job:

> "Finally, the most dismal bit – a wad of smallish paper money. I never even bothered with this item – the paper is still snug in its wrapper, untouched. Find some chips to use with the game.
>
> But please, no more paper money. It's hard to hide, flies around in a breeze, gets crumpled, worn and torn, and is generally really annoying for the banker."[118]

Fig.28 Paper Money from **Power Grid** *(Rio Grande, 2007)*

The usual recommendation is to replace it with counters, poker chips being a particularly common suggestion.

> "Well, speaking only for myself, there are a couple issues with paper money. People handle it a lot and it gets torn or wrinkled or folded. It only take one play to watch your stack of Power Grid money double in volume. It also tends to stick to itself and it makes it harder to tell if you are giving people the right amount of payout or change. Finally, its [sic] just seems to be faster to make change and pass the chips than it does to sort through the paper cash."[119]

The game even received a deluxe edition which replaced the paper money with plastic chips which might be a direct response to this criticism. Player's perceive paper money to be an inferior product, one not adequate to the task, and by implication its inclusion in older games is a sign of their inferior quality. This makes sense as a rationale because players who first started to play games in the wake of the euro-game craze tend to view component quality as one of the features that distinguish the euro-game from its predecessors[120].

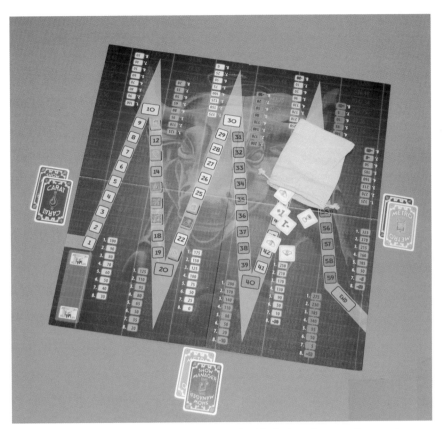

Fig.29 The 2013 edition of **Speculation** (Queen) with the board arranged as a price chart showing sharp rises and falls

This understanding – paper money is worse at its job, so implies low quality – helps to drive purchasing choices. Power Grid is a critically acclaimed game, probably the most well received of Friese's designs, but any game chasing sales at the height of the euro-game craze needed to conform. So, as an example Dirk Henn's Speculation which was first published in 1992, before the euro-game craze took hold, was subsequently re-released by Queen Games in 2013. It is a game about stock markets, whose graphic design originally resembled the bright multi-coloured look of a slot machine, and featured both dice and paper money.

In the re-design the board was aesthetically re-worked to resemble price charts showing rises and falls, bringing it closer to the trend for crash games that has dominated in the late twentieth century (see chapter 3), the dice were replaced with a clumsy draw-bag and tiles (which make it much longer to play), and the money was printed onto playing cards, still a representation of paper money but no longer paper money in the game. The game itself is essentially unchanged, but its aesthetic was brought in line with that which had come to dominate the euro-games.

However, while that insider perspective has helped to shape games, from academic point of view it feels unsatisfactory as an explanation of the cause. Modern board games had used paper money since 1903, yet no-one seemed to notice the problems that the critics of *Power Grid* take for granted. And this is not a cost or opportunity issue. Waddingtons were manufacturers

Fig.30 Cardboard coins from the television quiz-show tie-in game **For Love or Money** *(Chad Valley, 1959), which mixed both paper and coins*

of playing cards and could easily have substituted for paper money, as *Speculation* does, since all of the production facility was already in place. Companies like Chad Valley and Milton Bradley were toy manufacturers and had produced toy money, initially in board or card but subsequently in plastic, before they made modern games. On occasion an earlier game does in fact incorporate counters as money.

Yes, poker chips are probably ergonomically better (other than the obvious weight problems for transport), but euro-games did not substitute poker chips, they usually substituted card or board tokens that looked like coins. Those coins came to be associated with quality, which informed the understanding of players, and in turn shaped games like *Speculation*, but to get a fuller understanding of that we need a wider perspective.

Germany Loves Cash

"Whereas in most countries the choice of how to organise purchases is basically a question of utility, in Germany it's freighted with much deeper connotations."[121]

Bloomberg Markets, 2018

Let us begin by dealing with one obvious alternative reason for a preference for coins, theme. Euro-games, especially in the early 2000s showed a strong preference for themes based on European history from the medieval to early-modern period. Coins are a logical choice in those games because while banknotes existed from the fifteenth century onwards they were not that widely used until the nineteenth and twentieth. It is notable in this respect that some historic or fantasy games before the euro-game craze did use coins and that many stock-market games continue to use paper money. Theme clearly matters.

However, one of the earliest examples of a euro-game *Modern Art* (1992), does not have a medieval theme. With its fun pastiches

Fig.31 Cardboard counters from an early edition of Modern Art (Hans im Glück, 1992). Other editions employed plastic tokens, or in some cases coin designs.

of different twentieth century art styles it clearly positions itself in an art market in which payments, if made in cash at all, would be made using paper money, but the game uses counters. Specifically, round counters which are visually more reminiscent of coins than paper money. And this must be a deliberate choice, the publisher, Hans im Glück, had earlier used paper money for its games and nothing else in the game comes in the same die-cut format to justify it on efficiency grounds.

Euro-games originated in a German cultural context, a country whose preference for cash is often commented upon. Germans carry more of their money in a physical form than almost any other European nation, and more than most Americans. Various opinions have been expressed on why this is but a common explanation is that electronic transactions are traceable, depriving individuals of anonymity in a country where experiences of dictatorship make that a prized possession.

Will this do as an explanation for why euro-games tend to feature coins? Not really. The explanations tend to focus on a rejection of electronic rather than an embrace of physical money, they involve no preference for coins over paper. German preferences for cash seem to have diverged from other countries in the 1990s but it is unclear if this happened before the preference for coins became apparent in games.[122]. If German consumers do have a different sense of monetary value which drove the design of euro-games it goes deeper than a simple preference for cash.

The Gold Standard – Again

"There can be no doubt that the most stable system would be a 100 percent gold standard, in which banks cannot create fiduciary media at all and in which all forms of money represent claims to gold."

Detlev Shlichter, author of Paper Money Collapse

There is a genre of popular writing which focuses on apocalyptic economic collapse, and advocates the 'return' to gold as the only true medium for money. It enjoys very little respect from mainstream economists, a review in the *Financial Times* describing one such book as 'an entertaining prophesy that will convert few non-believers'.[123] I discussed in chapter 6 that *Dungeons & Dragons* and fantasy games in general feature gold coins as a unit of account, and it was notable that those games originated in America when that country abandoned the gold standard. Euro-games also frequently feature not just coins but specifically gold coins, even in games with a modern setting. *For Sale* received a 2005 republication which featured counters depicting silver ($1000) and gold ($2000) coins. One of these phenomena could be used to explain the other, perhaps fantasy games are simply so pervasive (at least amongst the sort of people who make games) that it was inevitable games would end up with variations on the ahistorical tri-metallic system of *D&D*. However, here I will suggest the relationship is subtle, that popular ideas of value, games of all sorts, and polemics advocating gold, in a world where money is changing rapidly, reinforce each other. This leads to a conception of 'real' value in which it would be unconscious and natural to use precious metal coins as symbolic representations of money. Germany is not exceptional in this, but for historical reasons is probably more receptive, which goes some way to explaining both a resistance to electronic money and the aesthetic choice of euro-games.

For simplicity I will focus on just one writer, James Rickards, and his book *The Death of Money*. Rickards argues that government mismanagement has resulted in a systemic problem which can resolve itself only with the collapse of our current monetary system, forcing a 'return' to a gold standard. Like most such writers Rickards uses claims of the widespread employment of gold coins in the past to make his argument:

> "Because of its purity, uniformity, scarcity, and malleability, gold is money nonpareil. Gold has been money for at least four thousand years ... King Croesus minted the first gold coins in Lydia, modern-day Turkey, in the sixth century BC ... anyone who rejects gold as money must feel possessed of greater wisdom than the Bible, antiquity, and the Founding Fathers combined."[124]

To unwrap this it is important to first of all understand the distinction between coins and standards, which Rickards is blurring. Gold coins are almost never made purely of gold. In antiquity they were almost always alloyed with silver and copper, sometimes for purely practical reasons of hardness but often to stretch limited supplies (a process known as debasement). The main difference between ancient precious metal coinage and modern coinage is that the value of the coin was related to its metal content, a coin which contained more gold was worth more. This is still broadly true, but it is easy to find examples today, such as the United Kingdom two pence and five pence coins, where the heavier coin is worth less, though both are now made of the same coated steel.

To distinguish between the practices terms such as 'token' or 'fiduciary' are used for modern coins, 'specie' or the misleading 'full-bodied' for ancient coins. Full-bodied is particularly misleading because ancient coins were almost always worth more than the metal they contained. They had to be because it was expensive to source the metals, run mints, distribute and manage the coins. To work as a monetary system the coins had to be worth at least that much more than the metal they contained. In fact since mints were often run at a profit rather than as a public good the coins would have been substantially over-valued.

While a gold coin is a physical representation of money a gold standard is a set of rules. Under such rules anyone who issues money, regardless of its form, is required to hold a certain amount of the standard. So, a government or bank might be allowed to print paper money but be required to physically hold an ounce of gold for every 18,000 dollar notes it prints. In principle the government or bank would guarantee to exchange gold for notes but unless a gold coinage was also employed that gold would be no more useful in paying for groceries that in it is today. [125]

Standards and coinages are in no way linked. India maintained a silver standard in the nineteenth century (issues of paper money required holdings of a certain amount of silver) but still had gold coins (the mohur in the north, the fanam in the south). For most of its history China operated no standards, issuing money on a flexible basis like modern governments, and that almost entirely in alloys of copper. In fact, gold coins have been historically comparatively rare, with most of history's long enduring coinages (the *shekel, drachm, denarius/penny, dirham, rupee, thaler/dollar*) being made in silver[126].

Rickards argues that gold is 'true money' and 'money was gold ... for four thousand years'[127], until governments and the IMF performed a confidence trick to pretend it was not. He believes fervently that gold possesses an inherent worth, an intrinsic value, which paper does not. This belief is what ties standards (properly speaking a matter for economists), coins (a numismatic issue), and Rickards prophecy together. Belief matters because in reality gold has no more intrinsic value than paper. You cannot eat it, it will not shelter you, or keep you warm. Broadly speaking money has always been made from things – gold, silver, copper, lead, paper, seashells – that do not provide the necessities of food, shelter, or warmth[128]. The world's most sophisticated pre-modern monetary system, based on a public accounting similar to modern cryptocurrencies, was operated on the island of Yap in the Pacific and used large donut shaped stones, often too large to move. None of these things ever really had intrinsic value, they were sustained by belief. Specifically, the belief that objects such as coins could be exchanged in the future for the necessities that the coins themselves cannot provide.

Gold matters if you believe in it. If you believe that gold is itself valuable it is that much easier to believe in a coin that contains gold, or a paper note whose issuer promises to exchange it for gold. Gold can lend its reputation for value and stability, warranted or otherwise, to the money it supports. So, of course, could silver or any other commodity. When belief in a monetary system fails the results are often spectacular, and disastrous, as Germany discovered during its hyper-inflation period in 1923. And perhaps the calls for a return to gold, for the use of gold coins, reflect a cultural unease – a lack of belief in paper, or government, or increasingly electronic accounts, as stores of value.

We have seen these ideas reflected in board games already. I discussed *Black Friday*, by Friedemann Friese who also designed *Power Grid*, in chapter 3. *Black Friday* featured a dual currency system, in which players can choose to earn one currency, which allows them to buy useful things in the game and improve their position, or to gain a second currency which is used to determine victory. This mechanic helps to create a tension, if a player collects the second currency too early they will be unable to take actions to improve their position during the game, if they wait too late they will be unable to buy enough of the second currency to win. This mechanic is not new, it is found in *Mine a Million*, first published in 1965. In *Mine a Million* one currency can develop mines or transport goods, and those goods can be sold for more of that currency or transported further to be sold for a different currency which is used only to determine victory points. Where the two games differ is in their presentation of the two currencies. In *Mine a Million* both are paper money, but the usable one is pounds sterling and the victory points are US dollars, while in *Black Friday* the usable one is paper money in general, and the victory points (true value) are silver and gold, represented by small bars.

Fig.32 Sterling and Dollar currencies from Mine a Million (Waddingtons, 1972, first published 1965), the former is to purchase services in the game, the latter to determine the winner.

Conclusion

Since 2001 the German government has been taking gold stored in New York, London, and Paris (the gold reserves of most countries are in practice stored abroad) and bringing it to Germany[129]. This repatriation is symbolic rather than practical, and like demands for a return to a gold standard, preferences for cash, or board games adopting coins and precious metals as their representation of value, it reflects popular attitudes towards money.

In all likelihood all of these disparate elements (game coins, preference for cash, movement of reserves) reflect a distrust, or a lack of comfort, with changes in money over the last century, but particularly in the last few decades. Just a hundred years ago the bulk of monetary transactions would have used physical objects, coins and notes, which are studied by the academic field of numismatics. Many of those coins contained some quantity of precious metal and a great deal of money was linked to precious metal standards. Today, the majority of transactions are electronic, based on accounting systems, and institutions and governments freely manipulate the total money supply without regard to an abstract standard. The move away from the physicality of money creates discomfort, particularly in countries like Germany where a shift from depending on abstract standards to depending on government and big business as guarantee of value raises uncomfortable historical memories.

Innovation in modern boardgames was concentrated for two decades in Germany. That was coincidental with changes in money in the late twentieth century but it does mean that games developed in this period reflect popular unease with the way money was changing. Euro-games in particular reflect this unease by casting back to an idealised picture of pre-modern money, one shared with, and probably influenced by, American role-playing games. Collectively all of the elements discussed here reinforce each other and can shape both our attitudes to money in the modern world and our understanding of money in the past. After all, more people reading this will have played a boardgame then have read a book on numismatics or gold standards.

8.
ALHAMBRA

"The Moors of Granada regarded the Alhambra as a miracle of art, and had a tradition that the king who founded it dealt in magic, or at least in alchemy, by means of which he procured the immense sums of gold expended in its erection."

Washington Irving, Novelist

Alhambra won the Spiel de Jahre in 2003. Players compete to build the most impressive version of the historic Spanish palace. The game has simple rules, uses cards and cardboard tiles drawn from a bag rather than dice, and players compete for resources or points but never directly attack each other, placing it firmly amongst the euro-games discussed in the last chapter.

The success of the game took some time. Dirk and Barbara Henn produced the first version together the gangster themed *Al Capone* in 1992, under their own company name db-Spiele. Dirk designed the game and his wife Barbara provided the art work. In 1998 the publisher Queen Games picked it up and released a stock market based version called *Stimmt So!* In that version players simply competed to have the majority of each stock. Finally it was published again as *Alhambra* with the stock replaced by cardboard tiles, representing different types of buildings, giving the sense that players were actively constructing something. Construction themes were popular at the time, in games like *Torres* (1999), *Carcassonne* (2000), or *Citadels* (2000), the first two of which also won the Spiel de Jahre.

Dirk Henn, whose other famous game *Wallenstein* is a depiction of the Thirty Years War, had not visited the Alhambra himself and did not come up with the idea for the theme. He had initially been struck by the idea of a game which used four different currencies while playing a conventional card game but what exactly you were buying was always up for grabs – the four currencies and the exact change problem we will discuss in a moment are the only constants. Queen Games knew their market well enough to realise construction and a medieval setting would help, but it was a friend of Henn's who suggested theming it around the thirteenth century Spanish palace.[130]

The central dynamic of *Alhambra* comes from its market. Each of the tiles in the market must be paid for in a different currency because, the game rules state, workers insist on being paid in their native currency. That of course is not true of the historical setting but it makes a certain intuitive sense, Muslim Spain was a complex cultural mix and craftsmen from many places would have worked on the palace. The money is represented by cards, with each card valued from 1 to 9 in four different currencies. Those currencies are represented by pictures of what appear to be coins intended to evoke the division between Christian and Islamic Europe, two have images with a pictorial element and European denomination names, two have images with no pictorial element using the names of denominations in the Islamic world. In fact only one is based on a contemporary coin, the *dirham* cards feature a picture of a double *dinar* issues by the Marinid dynasty who ruled in North Africa at the time. *Dirhams* are common silver coins, while double *dinars* are large gold coins, so even here the representation is quite loose. The games *dinar* is represented by a much later European medal showing alchemical symbols. The *ducat* card shows a gold coin from sixth century Iran and the *guilder* the centre of a seal from the French city of Dijon. At one time examples of all of these objects were held in the British Museum and so it is possible some early publication

*Fig.33 A Marinid double dinar and the a dirham card from **Alhambra** (Queen, 2003)*

inspired the designs[131].

In the game players use this money to buy parts for their palace, represented by cardboard tiles in several different types such as towers, arcades, or gardens. On each turn four tiles are offered in the market, and each sold for a different currency. To further complicate matters players do not receive any change. If the tile you want costs 7 dinars and you have cards worth 5 and 6 dinars then you will have to spend both and the tile will cost you 11. But Alhambra is just a game and this wrinkle exists simply to make things more complicated, doesn't it?

In 2002, the year before Alhambra was published, Thomas Sargent and François Velde published a book called *The Big Problem of Small Change*. In that book they turned their attention to the transformation of European currency in the thirteenth and fourteenth centuries – the period of the Alhambra's construction. Before this time most Christian European states had regularly minted only one denomination of coin, the silver penny, derived from a type and standard first established by Charlemagne (AD 742-814) but at the time the Alhambra was being built states had begun to increase the range of denominations.

There are obvious advantages to having a range of coin denominations, as we do today, because some denominations are more useful for certain tasks than others. You would not want to buy a television with pennies, while it would be awkward to buy a bag of sweets if the only denomination available was a high value bank note like a 20 or a 50. So today governments treat physical money as a public good and ensure a wide range of denominations are available for different uses. Medieval European governments broadly treated coinage as a revenue raising activity, they would set the rules and standards but would sell the right to make coins to a private individual who would then seek a profit from the activity.

The no change rule in *Alhambra* reflects a problem familiar to everyone in Northern Europe before the thirteenth century. A silver penny was a relatively small value, a worker might earn several in a day, but it was still significantly more than the price of a loaf of bread. In general small denominations are more versatile, you can pay a major expense with a lot of small coins but cannot pay a small expense with a single large coin unless you are willing to go without change. On the other hand large denominations are more convenient, you need to carry and count fewer coins. The silver penny strikes a good balance between these two.

However, from the thirteenth century Christian Europe began to do what Islamic states already did, produce multiple denominations, often in the same metal. The multiple denomination system is what the game represents, with each currency coming in denominations from 1 to 9. When you have multiple denominations the general public will show a strong preference for the smaller denominations for the reason already mentioned, you can pay a major expense with a lot of small coins. In *Alhambra* you can see this in the difference between a player who holds one card worth 9 dirhams or two cards worth 3 and 6 dirhams. Both allow you to buy any card costing 9 or less, but the first player is left with no cards, while the player holding two is left with one card if the tile costs 6 or less. The 9 pays exactly for only eight tiles in the game, while the 3 and 6 pay exactly for seventeen, so are more versatile. *Alhambra* players soon learn several sequences of numbers by heart:

1 2 4 6	2 3 4 6
1 2 4 7	2 3 4 7
1 2 4 8	2 3 4 8
Some useful sequences in Alhambra	

These six sequences are the only four card sets which allow a player to form every number between 2 and 13 (the range of prices for tiles) exactly. There are no hands of less than four cards which allow a player to pay for every tile precisely. They are all modifications of the geometric series 2^n (1, 2, 4, 8, 16 ...), and number sequences formed an important part of many euro-games, some of whose designers were mathematicians[132]. We might think of 1, 2, 4, and 8 as representing the ideal denomination set a government would issue for the *Alhambra* market. And in another of the coincidences that make *Alhambra* so interesting a few centuries later this is exactly the denomination system Spain adopted. Following a reform of the coinage in the sixteenth century the silver coins were divided into 1, 2, 4, and 8 reales, the 'pieces of eight' popularly associated with pirates.

However, in the real world, as Sargent and Velde pointed out, there is a problem with producing low denomination coins. The private individuals the government get to make coins were paid the same amount for turning a pound of silver into coins, regardless of what coins they make. The cost of making those coins – forming the blank pieces of metal, carving the dies with the design, or paying labourers – are the same regardless of the value of the final coin. When the only option is to make 240 pennies from a pound of silver there is no issue but if the mint has a choice it would be a lot less work to make 40 six-pence pieces. So the general public, like *Alhambra* players, will tend to prefer smaller denominations for their versatility, but the mint will want to make large denominations, leading to problems of supply.

In *Alhambra* players represent both sides of the equation. Instead of purchasing a tile for their palace a player can choose to take a money card from the market (effectively they act as the mint). In general 6, 7, or 8 cards are preferred to 9s,[133] but a player will not usually want to take a very low value card. Despite its flexibility taking a 1 rather than a 7 would make little sense, as the 7 can buy everything the 1 can. To compensate for this the player is allowed to take any number of cards if the total is 5 or less. So they can take a 1, a 1, and a 3, with the same action needed to take a single 9, and because of the greater flexibility of low denominations will often prefer to do so. Effectively the game has offered a discount on the production of small change to ensure that it gets into circulation.

In the real world it is much harder to solve the problem of small change than it is in a game and governments have continued to face shortages since the Middle Ages. In the seventeenth century the English government abandoned making small change entirely leaving it to private businesses to fill the gap with tokens; at the end of the First World War German small change failed leading to locally produced paper currencies. As recently as 2011 the Indian government was unable to provide small change and local market associations started supplementing with their own tokens.

Fig.34 One player's hand, their personal Alhambra, and the current market for money and buildings

In a final mirror of art and life, both Sargent and Velde's thesis and Dirk Henn's game have received some subsequent critical treatment. In addition to outlining the problem Sargent and Velde developed a mathematical model to explain the effects trying to provide a variety of denominations had. They used this model to argue that the system would always be unstable as long as the value of the coins was linked to the precious metal they contained. There model and the conclusions they drew have not won widespread support, as the numismatist Robert Tye put it

> "Despite being far too simple to mirror real events ... the model is simultaneously far too complicated for most readers (this one included), to easily assimilate ... I find it impossible to avoid the conclusion that the mathematical portions of the text often obfuscate rather than clarify the processes being described, and thereby tend to divert attention away from the historical errors."

Similarly Chris Wray[134], writing a retrospective review of *Alhambra* in 2015 for the website Opinionated Gamers questioned if the game would still win the Spiel de Jahre today, and several of the contributors to the Opinionated Gamers site bemoaned the over-complication that came with converting it from a simple stock market game to one about medieval construction. However the huge critical and commercial success *Alhambra* enjoyed compared to its earlier versions was probably a result of tapping the popular zeitgeist for medieval construction, and it did provide a layer of thematic justification to the 'exact change' mechanic.

9.
THE DARK(ER) SIDE OF BOARD GAMES

"... play is not just the ludic, harmless, encapsulated, and positive activity that philosophers have described. Like any other form of being, play can be dangerous; it can be hurting, damaging, antisocial, corrupting."

Miguel Sicart[135]

Historians do not look at pots solely to learn about potters or coins exclusively to understand how mints worked. Mundane objects are studied because they reveal important things about the wider societies in which they were made and used. It should be apparent by this point that a central argument in this book is that historians should interest themselves in modern games not because those games are fun or intrinsically interesting (though they are both of those things), but because they raise interesting questions about the societies that made them - primarily the United States, United Kingdom, and Germany in the mid to late twentieth century. And what they tell us is often not what they set out to say. Sometimes they reflect the darkest elements of human experience, and that is what this chapter is about.

By far the best-known example of this phenomena in the study of toys are the mechanical banks made in late nineteenth century America. These savings boxes were designed so a child could place a coin on a platform and then activate a mechanism which flipped, pushed, or tipped, the coin into the box itself. There is no question that mechanical banks were intended to encourage children to save by associating the activity with play, by making saving fun, but a substantial number of them are also racist caricatures of African Americans. The following advertising copy from 1907 suggests that nothing could be funnier for a small child than an accident befalling a member of a persecuted minority:

> "A most amusing bank, made of cast iron throughout. Place a coin in the rider's mouth and touch a spring. The mule's heels are flung up, the rider is thrown over the mule's head, and the coin is shot into the bank as the unfortunate nigger's head strikes the ground."[136]

This should not be a surprise. Toys generally seek to simulate, criticise, or educate us about, the world, and so they invariable reflect elements of the identity of the people who made them. The identity of Elizabeth Magie and her friends in Arden was wrapped up in their perception of economic exclusion which they saw as a function of landlordism, and they made a game about it. For other white Americans, personal identity was wrapped up in questions of race, and those prejudices are recorded in the mechanical banks. At the same time game and toy designers sometimes intended their creations to teach one thing but in practice the games were received in a very different manner. Magie did not intend for her game to appeal to people's base instincts, for example, yet it did.

The case of the makers of mechanical banks is not quite equivalent as the designers understanding of race are not being radically misinterpreted. However, the toys were intended as amusements to encourage saving, not as a method of perpetuating racial tensions. The disconnect between what designers intend, what players perceive, and the way a historian might read their cultural influence is interesting. These themes will be explored in this chapter first by delving into representations of particular dark moments in human history, including a system of economic exploitation, and then by asking if the disconnect fundamentally undermines the idea of educational games.

Game or Art-Installation?

"Train instils fear in me. It works on so many levels, answering so many questions about the potential of games as design and art, that it threatens to dominate any and all discussion of those questions."

Simon Ferrari, Research on Digital Media

Brenda Romero (formerly Brenda Brathwaite) is a video game designer who is best known for her non-digital series, *The Mechanic is the Message*, whose constituent parts could be described as either board games or art installations, or perhaps as both.[137] None of them are available commercially and players only have the opportunity to take part at organised events, often in galleries, supervised directly by the designer.

In *Train,* presented in 2009 and the third in the series,[138] players are asked to transport a certain number of yellow pawns from a loading point to a destination. They can load pieces onto the train, or roll a die to move the train, or take a card with some special event on it. Ostensibly the players are racing against each other though the rules are vague as to the end point or victory conditions. Despite the series title, *The Mechanic is the Message,* mechanically it is a simple race game and everything interesting is in the theme. The room is filled with clues but it is clearly expected players will only identify the theme of the game once the first journey is complete and a destination card is revealed. On those cards are written the names of concentration camps, making explicit that *Train* represents the events of the Holocaust.

Train has received a mixed response. Many academics, cultural commentators, and those involved with video games have accepted Romero's own framing of the game as exploring complicity within systems and responded positively to the central argument on the potential of games to transcend pure entertainment and engage with big issues. For advocates, *Train* demonstrates the capacity of games to be art, to move us and to make us think and question. Importantly, this argument is not directed at board games, rather *Train* acts as an analogy for an argument that is being made about video games – it does so in part by borrowing the clothes of traditional race games, which are often perceived to be entertainment for children.[139]

However, the response amongst those who play modern board games has been less universally appreciative. Though *Train* has found defenders, it has also elicited anger. This anger tends to focus on two distinct aspects: how it represents the Holocaust and its claimed status as a board game. Firstly, *Train* is a deception. Though players are given clues as to the general theme (broken glass, a typewriter of the period, the yellow pawns players are to transport) they require more than typical knowledge to identify the context. Romero, and many positive commentators, suggest that the game asks 'will we blindly follow the rules if we know where we are going'.[140] In fact it is only really asking if we can be tricked into doing something since most players immediately cease playing once the destination is revealed.[141] It seems we will not follow the rules if we know where we are going, but as critics point out perpetrators of the Holocaust did know, and carried on anyway. Critics also argue that the game acts as an apology for the crimes and distorts actual events.[142] As one commentator points out simply substituting the names on the destination cards for Tokyo stations would render it a rather dull simulation of overcrowding on urban infrastructure, so there is no sense in which the structure of the game communicates complicity with a system.

The second argument is that essentially *Train* is not really a board game at all, or as one online critic put it:

"What I object to most here is the willingness of a very skilled self-promoter to besmirch a perfectly acceptable and even social hobby by calling her product a game. This "Train" thing seems to me nothing other than a poorly designed, unsupervised and unlicensed social science experiment with some incidental historial [sic] references. While others may differ, there is nothing "game" like in her product -- the experimental subject makes no choices, there is no goal, there isn't really even any point to the exercise other than a decision to participate in the manipulation or not. That is NOT a game by any standard."[143]

The argument is that *Train* was never really intended as a game but uses board games to say offensive or controversial things the designer would not be able to say in her own field, and in the process it slanders a hobby in which the designer plays no part. The argument is strengthened by a comparison with the general release video-game *Playing History 2*. In that game a level was included in which players stacked slaves into a ship, and it produced a substantial negative backlash. Yet the design of that level shows striking similarities with the graphics Romero uses for the first game in her series, *The New World*, which also involves players packing slaves onto a ship.[144] What Romero does depends on analogy, and that analogy requires distance. By presenting her argument about video-games as a board game and then by presenting that as a unique object within a controlled museum environment she removes it sufficiently from the thing it makes an argument about to avoid any danger of offence. Of course, by overtly imitating another field that distance is collapsed for the players of board games that she offended.

The other issue implicit in this critique is that Romero does not understand board games. In her talks she references euro-games and designers in a way that suggests she is aware of and has played them, though she talks about older games such as *Monopoly* or *Candyland* in a manner that indicates she is unaware of the history[145]. As was seen in Chapters 1 and 2, modern board games frequently seek to satirise or comment on the real world. In fact they often began with exactly that goal in mind and drew on a tradition of nineteenth century games which focused on education. The kind of commentary which Romero is arguing video-games have the potential for has always been a central part of the board games she uses as analogy. And it should be no surprise that there is already a game about transporting Jewish people in the context of Nazi Germany. *Juden Raus*, named for an anti-Semitic slogan in Nazi Germany, was produced in 1938 and in the game players remove the Jews from a city and send them to Israel. It was a commercial game, intended to make money and provide entertainment. As with *Train* some players of boardgames have argued that it is disqualified from being a game by virtue of its subject matter:

> "at the point where a game ceases to be entertaining or fun then it ceases to be a game. At the point where a game becomes propaganda it therefore ceases to be a game and exists as a propaganda tool." [146]

At least for board games none of this speaks to the issue of complicity. After all no-one plays *Juden Ruas* today. And surely no-one would design, and if they did no one would play, a boardgame about horrific acts like the Slave Trade, would they?

An Answer to the Rhetorical Question

> "It feels disrespectful for Seyfarth to disregard slavery so completely. By using slavery as a gameplay mechanic without acknowledging the human cost of it (or even using its name directly), by rendering the institution to a mere tool, the true costs of running your economic engine are

ignored. It almost seems to uncritically adopt the slavers' mindset, without any self-awareness. The effect is to make players gathered around a table for a game of Puerto Rico into unwitting moral accomplices in the horrors of human servitude."

Sam Desatoff, Journalist[147]

Puerto Rico, published in 2002, is set during the colonisation of the New World, specifically the island of Puerto Rico and the development of the city of San Juan. The game is won by scoring the most victory points which are awarded for constructing buildings and for shipping goods (tobacco, coffee, corn, indigo, sugar) to Europe. Players take turns to select different roles which drive the game forward. They are described as follows (roles highlighted) in the games Spiel de Jahre nomination:

"**Settlers** make new fields arable and the **mayor** assigns to the players colonists who - driven by the **supervisor** to work - produce appropriate goods. The **master builder** in turn builds the buildings needed for production. For goods players get money from the **trader**, while the **captain** ships the goods to Europe, for which they are awarded victory points."[148]

Supervisor in the quote above is a literal translation of the German Aufseher. In English editions of the game this was role was rendered as 'craftsman'. The 'colonists' are represented by small brown discs which arrive by ship at the Island before being put to work by the players on their plantations. There is no question these represent slaves and the game is depicting two parts of the triangular trade with slaves arriving from Africa and goods being shipped to Europe.[149] The game does feature money, but this is used only for constructing the buildings, not for paying the 'colonists' or received for shipping goods to Europe. The designer, Andreas Seyfarth, has made clear in interviews that he develops games from particular themes, so presumably the game was always intended to represent the history of Puerto Rico.[150] It seems unlikely that the theme was simply superimposed on a fully developed set of mechanics late in the development.

Puerto Rico was critically acclaimed from its release, receiving many awards and a nomination for the Spiel de Jahre. Curiously it is the only year between 1996 and 2008 when the award is not won by something which could be described as a euro-game, in 2002 *Puerto Rico* missed the top spot to the dexterity game, *Villa Paletti*. For seven years *Puerto Rico* was the number one game on the ranking site Board Game Geek, despite the thinly veiled representation of slavery being almost immediately recognised by English speaking players.[151]

In many ways *Puerto Rico* provides a very interesting thought experiment when contrasted with *Train*, and is a much more interesting study in complicity. It is possible, as in *Train*, not to recognise the subject matter and to need it pointing out. It is possible, like *Train*, to refuse to play, or to sabotage the game. No new slaves arrive if a player refuses to take the Mayor role. It is possible to bypass the ship and get additional workers, but extremely inefficient, by using the Hospice and the University buildings. Exactly what the extra 'colonists' from the Hospice and University represent is not clear but they do not come from the ship distributed by the Mayor. This would be akin to the strategy sometimes reported in *Train* where a player refuses to move their own train and seeks to damage the tracks by playing cards. Unlike *Train* however it would require all players to cooperate in the disruption as *Puerto Rico* incentivises players to take roles others have rejected by adding a bonus doubloon each time all of the players pass.

Yet people do not engage in disruption or refuse to play and *Puerto Rico* is a popular game. I personally have played the game many times, and have never felt I should stop because of the theme or had any urge to sabotage the system whose simulation I am clearly complicit in. Yet I would not wish to play *Train*, or Romero's own slavery game *The New World*. Why the difference?

One obvious answer is that *Puerto Rico* is a much better game than *Train*. Perhaps if Romero had produced an engaging, challenging, and sophisticated modern game rather than a derivative race game, players would turn over the card revealing the destination and then insist on playing out the remaining turns. That seems unlikely. More likely it is about framing. Both games abstract and obfuscate the theme, but *Train* does so in order to subsequently shock the audience with the revelation. The game is framed by a context, museum spaces, where people expect a 'message' and it is distanced from its audience, as discussed above, to use analogy for difficult discussions.

Puerto Rico by contrast is abstracted because euro-games tend towards abstraction, it never uses that abstraction to set up a revelation, and as it is a commercial board game played by players of board games there is no distance to help set up an analogy. This might explain why academic response has been so muted. The very small number of academics who write about board games are usually also players of board games[152] as insiders they are likely to share the discomfort of players. For example Brian Mayer and Christopher Harris in their book *Libraries Got Game*[153] develop an argument that teachers should prefer commercial games to educational games because these represent 'authentic game experiences'. They then provide suggestions of suitable games and the topics they can teach. For example, *Power Grid* 'presents students with a sophisticated model of a market economy and some strong conversational points surrounding environmental science'. They do include *Puerto Rico* but recommend it only for teaching economics, the mechanical element of the game, and entirely ignore the theme. This is particularly ironic as both authors work in the United States, and it was Romero's experience of what her daughter learnt at school in the US about trans-Atlantic slavery which led her to develop her *Mechanic is the Message* series.

What the comparison of *Train* and *Puerto Rico* suggests is that Romero's argument does not really apply to board games, leaving aside whether it is a sound argument for video-games. Board games already tackle a wide range of difficult issues, from landlordism to slavery, and they always have, but they generally do not cause players to question those subjects. Even when, as in *Monopoly*, *Ratrace*, or *Class Struggle* we know games set out to question or satirise their own themes that does not seem to engage the players. In the normal context in which a board game is played, the players tend to accept game themes. It is only when games are re-framed in a different context, whether a museum or a classroom, or for the subject of critique as here, that they are engaged with differently. *Train* provokes its response because it is placed in a context where the audience expects to engage with what the game is about, rather than play it. *Puerto Rico* avoids provoking a response as it is usually encountered in the context of a social activity in which players do not expect to engage with weighty issues but rather to compete within the rules set by the game. The framing of the games acts as a narrative, which is why *Puerto Rico* can be about economics without engaging with colonialism or slavery, and why *Train* can be about complicity when nothing in the game itself addresses that point. The framing can apply its own narrative. Of course that doesn't tell us anything about what players take away from a game when it is played in its normal context.

Mayer and Harris therefore may be quite mistaken in their

argument that commercial games offer 'authentic game experiences'. The moment a game is framed by a classroom it is no longer being experienced the way it is by players who buy the games. In the next and final section we will compare two games, one commercial and one educational, which have been suggested as suitable for teaching about money, and ask how much utility either type of game really has.

Is Education Through Games Futile?

> "... the nature of games makes them vulnerable to abuse, particularly in the hands of inexperienced or lazy teachers. Used in isolation from books or discussion groups, the danger arises that games – most of which mirror political and economic institutions as they are – may encourage quiescent and conformist attitudes."
>
> *Elliot Carlson, 1967*

The use of games, both those designed for the classroom and commercial board games, as teaching aids, first became popular in the 1950s and 1960s in the United States. It is no coincidence that this followed the commercialisation of modern board games. Similarly, the renaissance in the popularity of board games which followed the euro-game craze has led to renewed interest in the teaching potential of contemporary board games. Yet there is a very real possibility that this is not only futile but potentially dangerous.

Warnings were given early in the development of educational games that they rarely teach what the tutor thinks they teach. Historically, almost every game I have written about here seems to reinforce the very things it set out to critique. Yet the field of educational games has blossomed to such an extent that publishers exist who provide games solely for schools, and a great deal of academic literature supports the use of modified commercial board games in the classroom. In this section we will look at two examples, one a recent commercial game and the other designed by academics as an educational game.

Tulipmania 1637, first published in 2009, was designed by Scott Nicholson. It falls firmly into the class of stock market games discussed in chapter 3 with a central grid like track for prices. It was partly inspired by *1829*, also discussed in chapter 3, but in general tone it is a crash game. Players attempt to sell their tulips when the market peaks and before the price collapses. Interestingly Nicholson suggests that it is a suitable vehicle for education:

> "Tulipmania can also work well as a game for the classroom. It can be used as a way of introducing the Tulipmania phenomenon and how bubble markets continue to this day. It can also be used to start a discussion about the role of speculators in investment. After playing the game, players can realise what power they had as a speculator to cause a market to rise. This can be used as a life lesson about following a trend when investing and realizing that sometimes speculators are making their own trend with the intention of selling off at the right time."[154]

It is worth noting that Nicholson had worked in library studies and does write about games in education,[155] so this blurs the line between commercial and educational a little, but what lesson does he expect players to learn from *Tulipmania*? Nicholson argues that speculators deliberately create rises or falls in markets in order to take advantage of naïve investors, or as the game suggests: 'make smart investments, artificially raise prices, fleece your network at the best time, and then make your escape from *Tulipmania* with the most money'.[156] This is a popular idea of how bubbles and crashes work,[157] going back to the seventeenth century when the game is set, but is it true?[158] As already noted in chapter 3 a common defence of speculation is that speculators actually perform a valuable role adjusting market prices, and some studies have argued they get swept up in bubbles along with everyone else, with luck more than skill distinguishing those who are caught by the crash.

As was also seen in chapter 3 stock market games tend to focus on the less salubrious interpretations of their subject – that it was reckless gambling, rife with illegal activity, or inevitably going to end in a crash – while mechanically requiring the players to engage in that same behaviour in order to win. In video-games this is sometimes called ludonarrative dissonance, where a player has to do one thing to win but the game's narrative suggests they should want to do something else. This tension is as old as modern board games. What makes *Tulipmania* unusual is that it resolves this tension by both mechanically and thematically advocating for players to steal and cheat. The game frames the market manipulation positively, not just as a victory condition but also by ridiculing those who 'invest foolishly' and celebrating the 'wily investor'. Did Nicholson design a game to act as advocacy for what are perceived as the worst behaviours of recent financial crashes? Is that the 'life lesson' intended?

Judging by comments made elsewhere, Nicholson understands the speculators in the game to be unethical, and has suggested that 'the overall lesson here is don't trust people with your money, ask why are they going to benefit from taking my money'.[159] Yet none of that has translated into the game. The game does not reward caution amongst the network of buyers, but rather the unethical behaviour of the speculators. Nor is there any sudden reversal or revelation, as in the art installation *Train*, which would suddenly bring into sharp relief the consequences of selling an over-priced tulip to an unsuspecting buyer. In fact

Fig.35 A note from the game Tulipmania 1637 (JKLM, 2008)

the game seems to minimise the ethical impact by reminding us that 'the bubonic plague was killing off 1 out of every 7 people per year, so the common man saw little reason not to invest foolishly with a good chance of making a substantial profit'.

Now seems a good moment to pause, as this feels slightly mean-spirited as a critique. *Tulipmania* is a commercial game intended primarily to act as entertainment. The designer's remark that you could employ it in a classroom is tangential to its main function. If it is an unfounded remark that is interesting, as is how often games do not match intent to effect, but it only becomes really interesting if games intended to teach fail with the same frequency.

Loy Loy, our second example, is specifically an educational game about financial institutions called RoSCAs. RoSCA, standing for Rotating Savings and Credit Association, is a term invented by anthropologists to describe a wide variety of different savings schemes found around the world but particularly well studied amongst low income groups in Africa and Asia. In a RoSCA, the members meet at regular intervals and at each meeting they contribute a certain amount to a common fund. The common fund is then allocated to one of the members, so that everyone receives a windfall once and pays in at all of the other meetings. The allocation method varies a great deal. In many groups there is an established order, with priority decided by when members joined or social status, or sometimes perceived need. In some groups allocation is done by drawing lots. Occasionally, though it is not the most common method, the members bid for the pot. Typically such a bid involves paying the other members who have not yet received a windfall.

How does a bidding RoSCA work?

RoSCAs in which participants bid are not particularly common but they are the type that most interest economists. Exact details vary enormously but a hypothetical example will suffice. Imagine that fifteen members of a RoSCA meet, and each contribute one hundred units to a pot. Three of the members have already received the pot at previous meetings so take no further part. The remaining twelve each secretly write down a bid on a piece of paper. Say that the winner bids fifteen units. The pot, worth 1500 units, is then given to the winner. That winner now has to pay each member, who has not previously received the pot, fifteen units, for a total of 165. So, the net effect is that the three members who have previously received the pot each paid 100; the eleven who lost the bid paid 85 each; and the winner made a net gain of 1235.

The classic economic justification of a RoSCA is that it acts as a loan allowing the members who receive money early to buy something expensive they cannot buy in parts, an indivisible good, quicker than they would be able to do so by saving. In this interpretation RoSCAs serve as informal financial institutions for people who cannot access bank or credit services. They undoubtedly can serve that function but RoSCAs also act as incentives to save, give security to the money, and operate as social clubs binding groups of people together.

Loy Loy seeks to simulate the classic economist understanding of RoSCAs in the context of urban Cambodia. Players represent women seeking to establish their own factory, for which they collectively need a certain amount of money (5000 loy). If the players acquire enough money in eight circuits of the board then the player who contributes the greatest amount wins. To illustrate the intent it is worth quoting from an academic paper by Qureshi, who had some involvement with the development:

> "Through role-play and in-game financial struggle, the game has the potential to serve as a postcolonial intervention, decolonizing growth and wealth ideologies by replicating financial behavior in a low-income society in the contemporary global South. ... *Loy Loy* holds promise as a financial education tool. It can encourage savings behavior and teach populations in the global North of the innovative, informal ways in which many people in the global South manage their money in contexts where access to formal financial services is limited or non-existent."[160]

These are grand ideas, the article juxtaposes its own objectives with the way commercial games, specifically *Settlers of Catan* and *Puerto Rico*, 'invoke and replicate a colonialist narrative'. Which makes it ironic that *Loy Loy* makes pretty much all of the same errors, but marries it to a more derivative and less entertaining version of a commercial game.

Loy Loy is based in large part on an educational game called *The Savings Game* which largely shares its mechanical structure with a commercial Waddington's game of the 1970s called *Pay Day*. In all of these games players complete circuits of the board. They may land on spaces which require them to meet expenditures, perhaps deferred until the end of the circuit. They also land on opportunities for investment. These cost money but earn a return later. For example, in *Loy Loy* a player might have the option to purchase a chicken for 30 loy, which will then earn them 10 loy each time a circuit of the board is completed. Since assets can be sold for half of their value at the end of the game any asset with a 25% or better return is worth purchasing if it will pay out twice; those with greater than 16.6% return if they will pay three times; and 10% returns (the worst in *Loy Loy*) if they will pay at least five times before the end of the game.

Loy Loy adds two elements to the basic structure used by *The Savings Game* and *Pay Day*. One is derived loosely from RoSCAs and the other from contemporary game design. Firstly, on each of the eight circuits the players have a RoSCA meeting at which they bid for a pot of money. In *Loy Loy* the lowest bid wins, and the player receives the amount of money they bid from each of the other players. This is a somewhat simplified representation of how such schemes actually work.[161]

The second element is that the game is 'semi-cooperative'. Some terminology is required. Pure cooperative games are games in which the players collectively win or lose as a team with no opponent where the game itself acts as a sort of puzzle. Reiner Knizia's highly regarded *Lord of the Rings* published in 2001 is a pure cooperative game but this type of game only became widely popular with the publication of *Pandemic* in 2007. Often a pure cooperative game is essentially a solitaire game being played by multiple people but some games depend on limited information for each player, such as *Hanabi*, published in 2010. They are complemented by what might be called traitor-cooperative games. In these a team of players is opposed by one, or more, player(s) often secretly trying to prevent them reaching their goal. Traitor-cooperative games are different from simple team games in that if you remove the 'traitor' the game would still play like a pure cooperative game, albeit probably quite an easy one. The first widely successful game of this type, *Shadows over Camelot*, was published in 2005.

Cooperative games have not been discussed in this book because they generally do not involve money, or economics. Firefighters, medics, people trapped on space ships, or submarines, assembling a fireworks display, on a quest, defending something, or solving a mystery, are all popular themes, but not economics. This is interesting in itself, as it would surely be just as dramatic for players to collectively play federal authorities attempting to stop the collapse of the financial system following a crash than it is to play the speculators blamed for it.

Loy Loy is not a cooperative game, though it incorrectly frames itself as such. It borrows a concept, the semi-cooperative game, which seems to have originated mostly as a marketing tool to attach the label used for a new, and popular, type of game to more conventional games.[162] For our purposes a semi-cooperative game is one in which the objective is still to win, but it is possible to have a draw involving all of the players.

To illustrate, imagine the final move of a game of *Loy Loy* with five players. Ann's combined cash and assets come to 2500, Ben's to 1200, Cat and Dec both have 1000, and Eli has 50. The combined wealth of the group, 5550, is more than the 5000 needed, so under normal circumstances Ann will win. However, imagine that Eli has an outstanding expenditure of 100. If a member of the savings cooperative goes bankrupt then the game ends in a draw. So it is in Ann's interest to gift Eli 50, which would prevent Eli going bankrupt but leave Ann enough money to win. However, Eli could refuse the gift forcing the game to end with a draw. Ann might of course offer more to try and persuade Eli, though never enough for Eli to win. The question of what Eli should prefer in terms of a draw, defeat, or various final positions, is a complicated issue that elicits strong feelings in the gaming community.[163]

The point is that semi-cooperative games have their own peculiar dynamic which derives from normative models of game play amongst those who treat it as a hobby. Broadly these dynamics favour Eli refusing a gift of 50 and taking a draw. Such normative models are probably not shared by people who do not play board games, or by Cambodian garment workers, most of whom would see a RoSCA as a purely co-operative activity, or at least one in which social obligation would make this sort of calculation unthinkable. What *Loy Loy* has done is to apply a developing world economist's gamified understanding of the transaction – winners and losers – to a context where those ideas are alien. This may not be the game's worst offence. RoSCAs are particularly interesting because they seem to spontaneously occur in groups without access to formal financial institutions. Academics trying to teach a version of RoSCAs super-imposed with the preoccupations of economists who use games culturally tied to the West, run the risk that the game might as Qureshi criticised commercial games 'invoke and replicate a colonialist narrative'. At the very least *Loy Loy* is certainly loaded with cultural and political messages the designers clearly did not intend.

Conclusion

This chapter has tried to pull together two of the main threads which run through the book in the context of some more substantial and weighty issues. The first of those threads is the argument that modern games are important, not just as an abstract study but because they raise interesting questions about the people who made them, and the people who play them. The second is the substantial gap that exists between what a game is designed to say about the world and what is understood by those who play it. It is hard to assess what players take from games but when games are examined closely they often seem to promote messages very different to those which were intended.

For those invested in games as a positive form of social engagement making them subjects of academic enquiry can be uncomfortable. Academic writing tends to reframe the objects of study in ways that can feel distorting or at odds with the experience of playing games, just like Romero's museum displays of *Train*. When studies involve a series of coincidences between *Alhambra* and medieval numismatics it feels relatively light hearted but when it poses the question of why we keep moving pieces in *Puerto Rico* long after we know they are slaves it becomes a much more serious introspection.

No-one should feel bad for playing a board game. Modern board games can be fun, they can be challenging, they can be an idle diversion, or an intellectual competition, and no analysis alters that experience. They are also deserving of analysis and they have interesting and important things to say about a wide range of subjects. Board games deserve to be treated as a serious subject of academic enquiry even, perhaps especially, by those who have no interest in playing them.

APPENDIX 1:
COLLECTING GAMES
AND TOY MONEY

"Maybe we could call our collecting of games as a form of a second childhood – transforming what began as a little hobby into a challenging addiction. But unlike many collectors who were seeking profit or prestige, our great satisfaction came from 'the hunt', and finding those very rare British boardgames that date from 1790 to about 1850."

Ellen Liman, British Games Collector[164]

It is traditional at the end of many numismatic books to include some comments on collecting and values. Readers interested in the collecting of modern board games will find valuable advice in Bruce Whitehill's catalogue of American Board games. Additionally, the collecting of denomination sets, which might appeal to collectors in the related field of toy money, has specific issues.

The main issue with assigning a value to a denomination set is that very few modern board games are actually worth anything. Examples of *The Landlord's Game*, until its acquisition by Parker Brothers when production increased into the hundreds of thousands, can fetch high prices. Almost everything else will not. Most modern commercial games sold hundreds of thousands of copies, and most contemporary players have little interest, for reasons touched on in chapter 6, in games before 1990. There are a few exceptions. A copy, in good condition, of an early example of Sid Sackson's *Acquire*, would cost quite a bit more than a new game but such games are purchased to be played. Some games of much lower quality, especially those themed around movies or pop culture, will fetch higher prices because they appeal to collectors interested in the theme.

Otherwise even a first edition of *Totopoly*, or an early edition of *Buccaneer*,[165] both eminently playable games, with considerable nostalgic value and interesting historical artefacts, are to be had from flea markets or second hand sales for £10-20, about a quarter of what a game with similar production values would cost today.[166] Most games could produce a large number of denomination sets, so would those then be worth just a small fraction of the already modest prices of the games. The British Museum's collection was not purchased: they are all gifts, often from Museum staff. As Ellen Liman suggests above, the pleasure donors derived from expanding the collection came from 'the hunt' – including disrupting one very serious meeting on UK museum collections with several enthusiastic numismatists hunting the errors in the Imperial script on Star Wars themed money.

So I will leave you with one final game, for which collecting a denomination set is an unusual challenge. *Prosperity* is a *Monopoly* derivative produced in 1986 by its designer Mark Caines. The paper notes in the game come in six denominations, each produced by a different coloured ink on white paper and featuring a hand drawn image of the Victorian engineer Isambard Kingdom Brunel and the Clifton Suspension Bridge.

The notes are playful in the way much game money is, with the designer credit included in the position of the cashier's signature, but these notes take that playfulness a little bit further. You should hopefully spot that on some notes Brunel is wearing sunglasses. In fact there are eight small variations on the original design, presumably produced as a single sheet and then cut by a printer. Together the notes form an elaborate spot-the-difference puzzle, can you find the eight differences, and which of the notes must be the original base design?

Presumably the notes would have been delivered by a printer in stacks with identical designs and it would be necessary to manually mix them before parcelling sets out into individual games, a task prone to errors. A complete set would contain 48 notes (6 denominations, 8 designs) but the British Museum has a donation from only one copy of the game, and thus just 21 distinct notes.

Fig.36 The eight designs used for notes in the game Prosperity (Casper, 1986)

APPENDIX 2:
SUGGESTED READING
ON PLAY AND GAMES

While modern board games are not extensively studied the concept of play has been of great interest to both philosophers and anthropologist. Foundational are the works of Jacob Huizinga (1872-1945) and Roger Callois (1913-1978). Jacob Huizinga's *Homo-Ludens: A Study of the Play-Element in Culture*, was based on a lecture he gave in 1933 and was first published in Dutch as *Homo Ludens: Proeve Eener Bepaling Van Het Spel-Element Der Cultuur*. There have been many English editions based on notes by Huizinga and a 1944 German edition, translated by R.F.C Hull, and first published by Routledge & Kegan Paul in 1949. Huizinga offers a definition of play (rather than games) and as a historian is mostly concerned with how the 'play-form' (*spel-element*) underpins culture. Roger Callois' *Man, Play and Games*, translated by Meyer Barash in 1961 from *Les jeux et les hommes*, first published in 1958, has also been extensively reprinted. Caillois is also concerned primarily with defining 'play', and like Huizinga he has little interested in board games. In fact Huizinga is particularly dismissive of board and card games when he does speak of them. Despite this the definitions of play developed by Huizinga and Caillois, particularly the idea that it occupies a limited space distinct from other activities, sometimes referred to as the magic circle, have been very influential on the study of game design, see for example Katie Salen & Eric Zimmerman, *Rules of Play: Game Design Fundamentals*, MIT Press, 2003.

However there is very little literature on the history of board games, and particularly for modern board games. Traditional games are best served, the still important work by Charles Murray in 1952, *A History of Games other than Chess*, has had many successors. The most comprehensive and up to date being David Parlett's *Oxford History of Board Games*. *Monopoly* is better served than most with the most accessible account being the 2015 book by Mary Pilon, *The Monopolists*. Accounts by Orbanes and Anspach suffer from the close involvement of both authors in the legal disputes around *Anti-Monopoly*.

No detailed account has been published of the period of games history after the success of Monopoly in the 1930s, and no detailed history of any of the major manufacturers other than Parker Brothers. Most books covering this period are simple catalogues listing games that were published. The best of these is Bruce Whitehill's *American Boxed Games* in 1992, which can be usefully supplemented by many of the chapters in Donovan's 2017 *It's All a Game*, each of which focuses on a specific game. The period after 1990 is better served as the opening chapters of Stewart Woods' *Eurogames* contains a relatively detailed history.

Modern board games represent only a small section of what are sometimes called games of skill or table top games. On topics related to the games covered in this book Gerda Reith's *Age of Chance*, is a particularly interesting and well-regarded account of the development of gambling in the modern western world. It provides a solid bibliography on that quite substantial field. Likewise Jon Peterson's *Playing at the World* provides a very detailed account of the development of role-playing games, which also has a fairly substantial literature.

BIBLIOGRAPHY

Abbreviations

BGG   References to the games in the Board Game Geek database are given as numbers, URLs can be formed by appending them at the end of https://board gamegeek.com/board game/. For example BGG 15343, the game *Frenzied Finance,* corresponds to https://board gamegeek.com/board game/154343.

WYC   Archives of Waddingtons held by the West Yorkshire archive service in Leeds. Numbers refer to the deposit and box number but note that numbers are frequently duplicated within the archive.

Books and Articles

Acton, R. 1990. 'A Colonial Childhood: Coming of Age in Rhodesia' *The North American Review*, vol.275, no.2, 9-14

Adams, D.W., Edmonds, V. 1977. 'Making your move: The educational significance of the American Board game, 1832 to 104' *History of Education Quarterly*, vol.17, no.4, 359-383

Ansoms, A. Geenen, S. 2012. 'DEVELOPMENT MONOPOLY: A Simulation Game on Poverty and Inequality' *Simulation & Gaming*, vol.46, no.6, 853-862

Banner, S. 1998. *Anglo-American Securities Regulation, Cambridge University Press*

Barton, C.P. & Somerville, K. 2012 'Play things: children's racialised mechanical banks and toys, 1880-1930' International Journal of Historical Archaeology, vol.16, no.1, 47-85

Baudelaire, C. 1853. 'The philosophy of toys', reprinted in I. Parry & P. Keegan (Eds.), *Essays on dolls.* London: Syrens, 1995.

Beers, L.D. 2010. 'Punting on the Thames: Electoral Betting in Interwar Britain' *Journal of Contemporary History*, vol.45, no.2, 282-314.

Bell, R.C. 1960/69. *Board and Table Games from Many Civilizations*, Oxford University Press, 2 vols. [reprinted and bound as single volume by Dover Press, 1979]

Bloomfeld, D. 2012. 'Central Banking in Middle-Earth, or: The much-maligned King Thror' 20 Dec 2012 https://mortonandgeorge.wordpress.com/2012/12/20/central-banking-in-middle-earth-or-the-much-maligned-king-thror/

Blum, J. 1986. 'The regulation of insider trading in Germany: Who's afraid of self-restraint' *Northwestern Journal of International Law & Business*, vol.7, no.3, 507-31

Boeschoten, W.C. & Fase, M.M.G. 1989. 'The Way We Pay with Money' *Journal of Business & Economic Statistics*, vol.7, no.3, 1989: 319-26

Borit, C. . Borit, M., and Olsen, P., 2018. 'Representations of Colonialism in Three

Popular, Modern Board Games: Puerto Rico, Struggle of Empires, and Archipelago', *Open Library of Humanities*, 4, 17, 1-40

Braggon, F., Moore, L. 2012. 'How insiders traded before rules' Discussion Paper 2012-007; http://lyndonmoore.yolasite.com/resources/Insider%20Trading.pdf

Braithwaite, B. & Sharp, J. 2010. 'The Mechanic is the Message: A Port-Mortem in Progress' in Schrier, K. Gibson, D. (eds) *Ethics and Game Design: Teaching Values through Play*, 311-329

Brewster, P.G. 1953. *American Non-Singing Games*, University of Oklahoma Press

Brown, M.E. 1979. "Academic freedom in the state's university: The Ollman case as a problem for theory and practice", *New Political Science*, vol.1, no.1, 30-46

Callois, R. 1958 *Man, Play and Games. Trans. Barash, M., University of Illinois Press [2001 edition]*

Campbell, G., Turner, J.D. 2012. 'Dispelling the Myth of the Naive Investor during the British Railway Mania, 1845—1846' *The Business History Review*, Vol. 86, No. 1, 3-41

Campbell, J. 1949 *The Hero with a Thousand Faces*

Campbell, M. 2018 'Germany is still obsessed with cash' *Bloomberg Markets*, 6 Feb 2018, https://www.bloomberg.com/news/features/2018-02-06/germany-is-still-obsessed-with-cash

Campbell, T.C. 2016. 'Putting the "Real" in Real Options: A Board Game Approach' *Journal of Financial Education*, vol.42, no.1-2, 102-115

Carreiro, J.L., Kapitulik, B.P. 2010. 'Budgets, board games, and make believe: the challenge of teaching social class inequality with non-traditional students' *The American Sociologist*, vol.41, no.3, 232-48

Cassidy, R. 2009. "'Casino capitalism' and the financial crisis" *Anthropology Today*, vol.25, no.4, 10-13

Castranova, E. 2014. *Wildcat Currency: How the Virtual Money Revolution is Transforming the Economy*, Yale University Press

Chartres, J.1 1993. 'John Waddington PLC, 1890s to 1990s: a strategy of quality of innovation' in Chartres, J. Honeyman, K. (eds.) *Leeds City Business*, Leeds University Press, 145-185

Coghlan, C.L., Huggins, D.H. 2004. 'That's not fair? A simulation exercise in social stratification and structural inequality' *Teaching Sociology*, vol.32, 177-87.

Costikyan, G. 2011. 'Board game Aesthetics' in Costikyan, G., Davidson, D. (eds.) *Tabletop: Analog Game Design*, ETC Press, 179-186

Crampton, E. 2012. 'Best not to leave a live dragon out of your calculations' 31 Dec 2012 https://offsettingbehaviour.blogspot.com/2012/12/best-not-to-leave-live-dragon-out-of.html

Dee, S. 2016. *Ticket to Carcassonne: 21st Century Tabletop Games.*

Desatoff, S. 2017. 'How Board Games handle slavery' *Waypoint,* 14 May 2017 https://waypoint.vice.com/en_us/article/vvj39m/how-board-games-handle-slavery

Deterding. S. 2015. 'The Mechanic is not the (whole) message: procedural rhetoric meets framing' *Train* & *Playing History 2*'Proceedings of 1ˢᵗ International Joint Conference of DiGRA and FDG

Donovan, T. 2017. *It's All a Game: The History of Board games from Monopoly to Settlers of Catan,* New York.

E-Crunch Ltd 2014. 'The Dragon Economy: How Smaug's death doomed Middle-earth' 11 Apr 2014, https://www.crunch.co.uk/knowledge/expertise/dragon-economy-smaugs-death-doomed-middle-earth/

Ender, M. G. 2004. 'Modified monopoly: Experiencing social class inequality' *Academic Exchange Quarterly,* 8, 249-254.

Erasmus, C.J. 1950. 'Patolli, Pachisi, and the Limitationof Possibilities' in Avedon, E.M. & Sutton-Smith, B. (eds.) *The Study of Games,* John Wiley & Sons, 1971 [first published in *Southwestern Journal of Anthropology,* 6, Winter, 1950, 369-87]

Ernest, J. 2011. 'Strategy is Luck' in Selinker, M (ed.) *Kobold Guide to Board Game Design,* Open Design, 61-5

Fatsis, S. 2002. *Word Freak,* Yellow Jersey Press.

Ferrari, S. 2011. 'Train' in Costikyan, G., Davidson, D. (eds.) Tabletop: Analog Game Design, ETC Press, 146-157

Fisher, E.M. 2008. 'USA Stratified Monopoly: A Simulation Game about Social Class Stratification' *Teaching Sociology,* vol.36, no.3, 272-282

Galbraith, J.K. 1954. *The Great Crash 1929,* 1954 [Penguin, 1987 edition]

George, H. 1879. *Progress and Poverty: An Inquiry into the Cause of Indutrial Depressions and of Increase of Want with Increase of Wealth, The Remedy,* [2017 reprint of Doubleday, 1912, edition]

Groot, F. de Voogt, A., Retschitzki, J. 2004 *Moves in Mind: The Psychology of Board Games,* Taylor and Francis

Harrison-Walker, L.J. 2002. 'If you build it, will they come? Barriers to International e-Marketing' *Journal of Marketing Theory and Practice,* vol.10, no.2, 12-21

Hockenhull, T. 2015. *Symbols of Power, Ten Coins that Changed the World,* British Museum Press

Hoffman, A.R. 2017. *Georgian and Victorian Board Games: The Liman Collection,* Pointed Leaf Press

Horn, F. & de Voogt, A. 2017. 'The Development and Dispersal of L'Attaque Games' in Silva, J. N. (ed.) *Board game Studies Colloquim XI,* Lisboa, 43-52

Huber, J. 2014. 'How Acquire became Acquire' *The Opinionated Gamers https://opinionatedgamers.com/2014/05/29/how-acquire-became-acquire/*

Huizinga, J. 1938 *Homo-Ludens: A Study of the Play-Element in Culture*

Jessup, M.M. 2001. 'Life on the boardwalk' *Teaching Sociology*, vol.29, no.1, 102-9

Jones, C. 2017. 'Germany repatriates gold stashed abroad during cold war' *Financial Times*, 23 August, 2017, https://www.ft.com/content/813c5460-87f9-11e7-bf50-e1c239b45787

Larimore, C. 2012. 'The Problem of Greed in JRR Tolkien's The Hobbit and The Lord of the Rings' in *Plaza: Dialogues in Language and Literature* 2.2, 2012, 64-70

Laybourn, K. 2017. *Working-Class Gambling in Britain, c.1906-1960s: The Stages of the Political Debate*, Edwin Mellen Press, 2017

Lehdonvirta, V. & Castronova, E. 2014. *Virtual Economies: Design and Analysis*, MIT Press

Levy, R.C., Weingartner, R.O. 1990. *Inside Santa's Workshop: How Toy Inventors Develop, Sell, and Cash in on their Ideas*, Henry Holt & Company: New York

Lewis, M. (ed.) 2008. *Panic! The Story of Modern Financial Insanity*, Penguin.

Logas, H.L. 2011 'Meta-Rules and Complicity in Brenda Brathwaite's Train' *Proceedings of DiGRA 2011 Conference*

Mackintosh, J. 2014. 'Review of The Death of Money by James Rickard', *Financial Times*, 6 April 2014, https://www.ft.com/content/b0c92908-bb3b-11e3-948c-00144feabdc0.

Mahoney, P.G. 2003. "The Origins of the Blue-Sky Laws: A Test of Competing Hypotheses" *The Journal of Law and Economics*, vol.46, no.1, 229-251

Manne, H.G. 1966. *Insider Trading and the Stock Market*, Free Press

Mayer, B., Harris, C. 2010. *Libraries Got Game: Aligned Learning through Modern Board Games*, American Library Association.

McKibbin, R. 1979. 'Working-Class Gambling in Britain 1880-1939' *Past & Present*, no.82, 147-178

Moore, K. 1997. *Museums and Popular Culture*, Leicester University Press

Murray, H.J.R. 1952. A History of Board Games Other than Chess, Oxford University Press

Neal, L. 2011. 'The Evolution of Self- and State Regulation of the London Stock Exchange, 1688-1878' in Ma, D., Luiten van Zanden, J., *Law and Long-Term Economic Change A Eurasian Perspective*, Stanford, 300-322.

Noer, M. 2012. 'How much is a dragon worth, revisited' 23 April 2012, https://www.forbes.com/sites/michaelnoer/2012/04/23/how-much-is-a-dragon-worth-revisited/#21a768c3f550

O'Sullivan, M. 2007. 'The Expansion of the U.S. Stock Market, 1885-1930: Historical Facts and Theoretical Fashions' *Enterprise & Society*, vol.8, no.3, 2007, 489-542

O'Toole, C.A. 1967. 'Monopoly in the Classroom' *The Clearing House*, vol.42, no.3, 145.

Ollman, B. 1983. *Class Struggle is the Name of the Game: True Confessions of a Marxist*

Businessman, William Morrow and Company, 1983.

Orbanes, P.E. 2003. *The Game Makers: The Story of Parker Brothers from Tiddly Winks to Trivial Pursuit,* Harvard

Parlett, D. 1999. *The Oxford History of Board games,* Oxford University Press

Parlett, D. 2007 'Games & Puzzles: The inside story' http://www.parlettgames.uk/gamester/gamespuz.html, downloaded Nov 2018

Patrick, K.G. 1972 *Perpetual jeopardy: the Texas Gulf Sulphur affair, chronicle of achievement and misadventure,* MacMillan

Paino, M., Chin, J. 2011. 'MONOPOLY and Critical Theory Gaming in a Class on the Sociology of Deviance' *Simulation & Gaming,* vol.42, no.5, 571-588

Peterson, J. 2012. *Playing at the World: A History of Simulating Wars, People and Fantastic Adventures, from Chess to Role-Playing Games,* Unreason Press

Pilon, M. 2015. *The Monopolists,* Bloomsbury.

Polizzi, R., Schaefer, F. 1991. *Spin Again: Board Games from the Fifties and Sixties,* Chronicle Books

Qureshi, F. 2018. 'Simulating the Community Bank: Postcolonial Capital, RoSCAs and Game Design' *Analog Game Studies* 3

Rateliff, J.D. 2007. *The History of the Hobbit,* Harper Collins, 2007

Reith, G. 2002. *Age of Chance: Gambling and Western Culture,* Routledge

Rickards, J. 2015. *The Death of Money,* Penguin

Salen, K., Zimmerman, E. 2003. *Rules of Play: Game Design Fundamentals,* MIT Press, 2003.

Schlichter, D. 2011. *Paper Money Collapse: The Folly of Elastic Money and the Coming Monetary Breakdown.* John Wiley & Sons.

Shanklin, S.B., Ehlen, C.R. 2007. 'Using The Monopoly Board Game As An Efficient Tool In Introductory Financial Accounting Instruction' *Journal of Business Case Studies,* vol.3, no.3, 17-22

Sharp, J. 2015. *Works of Game: On the Aesthetics of Games and Art,* MIT

Sicart, M. 2014. *Play Matters,* MIT

Sackson, S. 1969. *A Gamut of Games,* Hutchinson

de Sola Rogers, D. J. 1990. *Toy Coins,* Galata Print

Steiner, P.O., Rosenbaum, R.A. 1979 'Academic Freedom and Tenure: University of Maryland.' *Academe: Bulletin of the AAUP,* vol. 65 no. 4, 213-27

Stevens, H., Pers, W. 1998. *Dutch Enterprise and the VOC, 1602-1799*

Strange, S. 1986 *Casino Capitalism*

Swain, C. 2010. 'The Mechanic is the Message: How to Communicate Values in Games through the Mechanics of User Action and System Response' in Schrier, K.

Gibson, D. (eds) *Ethics and Game Design: Teaching Values through Play*, 217-235

Tolkien, C. 1996. *The History of Middle Earth: Vol. 12 The Peoples of Middle Earth*, Harper Collins

Walker, B. 1988. 'Essen Games Fair: 27th – 30th October 1988' Games International 2, 30-33

Walters, B.L. 1988. 'The Lean Years: John L.Casteel's Diaries, 1931-1942' *Oregon Historical Society*, vol.89, no.3, 229-301

Waren, W. 2011. 'Using Monopoly to Introduce Concepts of Race and Ethnic Relations' *Journal of Effective Teaching* 11, 1, 28-35

Whitehill, B. 1992. *Games: American Boxed Games and their Makers, 1822-1992, with values*, Chilton Book Company: Pennsylvania.

Wittgenstein, L. 1953. *Philosophical Investigations*, [trans. Anscombe G.E.M.; Hacker, P.M.S; Schulte, J. revised 4th edition, Wiley-Blackwell 2009]

Woods, S. *Eurogames: The Design, Culture and Play of Modern European Board Games*, McFarland, 2012

Woolley, F. 2012 'The Macroeconomics of Middle Earth', 30 Dec 2012 https://worthwhile.typepad.com/worthwhile_canadian_initi/2012/12/the-macroeco.html

Vohs, K.D. Mead, N.L. Goode, M.R. 2006. 'The Psychological Consequences of Money' *Science*, vol.314, no.5802, 1154-1156

ENDNOTES

1   Baudelaire 1853, 1

2   A general catalogue of toy money, de Sola Rogers 1990, which draws in part on the British Museum collection already exists.

3   BGG 34720, also locatable in the British Museum's Collections Online, https://www.britishmuseum.org/research/collection_online/search.aspx with the registration number, 2008,4006.1

4   Critiques like this are often directed at museums, see for example Moore 1997, 136.

5   Primarily as parts of the collections donated by Dr Freudenthal (1870) and Mr Parkes-Weber (1906).

6   Laurie and Whittle's *New Moral & Entertaining Game of the Mansions of Happiness* was published in 1800, see Hoffman 2017, 48.

7   Information on this early game is frustratingly sparse. Orbanes 2003, 4ff, gives a few details and in describing its central mechanic mentions the game *War*. *War* is a generic name for a class of games of which the more sophisticated *Top Trumps* series are probably the best known examples, but exactly how this worked with the 'loan' and 'speculation' elements Orbanes refers to is unclear.

8   Adams & Edmonds 1977, 377ff.

9   Scott, A. 'A shouting human can sometimes be more effective than a computer' *Market Place*, Jan 2017, https://www.marketplace.org/2017/07/13/business/chicago-open-outcry

10 It could be argued that the traditional card game *Commerce*, not to be confused with the commercial game of the *Bourse* type that uses the same name, has a connection between its trade theme and the mechanic of exchanging cards with a face up central 'market'. As the early history of the *Bourse* games is unclear, it is possible they derived from a traditional card game of some sort.

11 *Pit* (BGG 140), *Bourse* (BGG 202987), *Commerce* (BGG 26922), *Gavitt's Stock Exchange* (BGG 201147), *Panic* (BGG 195383)

12 To illustrate the dispute, at the time of writing the BGG entry (BGG 140) for *Pit* includes the following text in its description, 'Pit's designer, noted psychic Edgar Cayce, is often accused of having stolen the idea from the game Gavitt's Stock Exchange (G-S-E) invented by Harry Gavitt. While G-S-E claimed patents dating as early as 1896, it involved trading railway shares, and was only copyrighted and published in 1903, the same year as Pit. In addition, the only related patent assigned to Gavitt is US746492 A, filed October 7, 1903, and granted December 8, 1903. Also hitting the market in

1903 was Bourse, a remarkably similar open-outcry commodity trading game from Flinch Card Co., using an 80-card deck with 10 each of 8 commodities, and Panic, using a 65 card deck with 8 each of 8 commodities and a Panic card, roughly equivalent to the Bull. Pit, however, seems to have cornered the market on open-outcry games, as neither of its competitors were seen again after 1904.'

13   The note in the *Hopkinsville Kentuckian*, vo.XXV, no.80, 9 Oct 1903, 3, reads as follows, 'Mr Edgar Cayce, head clerk in the bookstore of L.D.Potter & Co., on State street, is the author of a parlor game which will net him considerably money and bring him much fame. The name of the game is "The Pit," and is to be played with a deck of sixty-four cards. It is on the order of the famous game of "Bourse" but those who have played both games say that the one of which Mr. Cayce is the author is far superior to the other. The cards represent the various cereals, railroad, mining stock, etc., which are sold by the New York exchange. They are first dealt to the players and the object is to corner the market, on certain things. The one doing this the winner. To play the game successfully requires considerable science and luck of course players no small part. Mr. Cayce has sold his game outright to the Parker Manufacturing Co., of Salem Mass. He received a good price for it and is naturally quite elated over its success. The game will be placed on the market as soon as a copywright [sic] can be procured.".

14   O'Sullivan, 2007.

15   *Frenzied Finance* (BGG 15343); and *Trusts and Busts* (BGG 37199).

16   George 1879, Part III: Recantation, Ch. XI Compensation.

17   BGG 5393

18   Pilon 2015, 61ff

19   That battleship was widely played by the time Murray published is clear because it is included in Brewster 1953, which was largely based on informants during the1940s.

20   Bell 1960/69, 69-70, corrected Murray's oversight by including an ancestor of *Stratego* under the title The Jungle Game. Though Jacques Johan Moggendorf is credited with creating *Stratego* it is a direct adaption of *L'Attaque* which was patented by Eden in France in 1909 (patent no. 396,795). Horn & de Voogt 2017 briefly discuss the history and suggest an even earlier patent, 1907 may have existed.

21   Adams & Edmonds 1977, 376.

22   I receive $7 each time another player lands on the space, but one of the other players also loses $7. So on average I gain an advantage of $9.33 (7 + 7/3) relative to the other three players (assuming other players land on my space with equal frequency). After seven occasions my relative gain is just over $65, which is slightly less than the $70 I originally paid, and after eight it is just under $75, a net gain on the original investment.

23   Contemporary designers take it for granted that all games consist of some mixture of strategy and luck, see for example Ernest 2011.

24   A board survives marked 'Economic Game Company of New York', and since it uses the patent number was made before 1921 (US Patents at the time expired after 17 years). A version was published in Scotland under the title *Brer Fox and Brer Rabbit*, shortly after the Second World War. Unfortunately a comprehensive academic catalogue of early boards is lacking which makes tracing the precise early development difficult, though a number of early boards are collected at http://landlordsgame.info/.

25   Both names appear on a patent Magie filed in 1924.

26   We know for example that Magie offered it to Parker Brothers, as did others, and likely to other companies. Several other versions eventually made it to market, as *Finance, Inflation,* or *Easy Money* and likely they were offered to several publishers first. However Parker Brothers is the only company to have received a detailed history and therefore it is hard to say how many offers other companies received in this period.

27   Levy & Weingartner 1990, 251.

28   This misunderstanding of the game seems to have developed very early, a diary entry from May 30, 1936 reads "Tonight, we were down to Clark's to play 'Monopoly'. This is a game that has had some recent, faddish popularity. It was invented by a man who supposed that since people in these times had no money, they would enjoy playing at it... The game is exciting, but it appeals to the acquisitive instinct: I doubt whether it can last." Walters 1988, 229-301

29   S. 1990 — 98th Congress: Trademark Clarification Act of 1983." www. GovTrack.us. 1983. June 22, 2018 https://www.govtrack.us/congress/bills/98/ s1990.

30   As recently as 2013 Hasbro's lawyers were able to block a religious themed game called *Galatopoly*, http://ipkitten.blogspot.com/2013/10/the-monopoly-of-opoly-no-revelations-in.html (Jun 2018).

31   Dee 2016, 10. To illustrate this dislike Dee 2016 contains a rather mean-spirited short story at the back intended largely to denigrate *Monopoly*.

32   The idea of using *Monopoly* for education is quite old, see O'Toole 1967, and there is a substantive literature on using it for teaching about social and economic and inequality, see publications by Jessup 2001, Coghlan & Huggins 2004, Ender 2004, Fisher 2008, Paino & Chin 2011, Waren 2011, Ansoms & Geenen 2012, though much of this is problematic for reasons discussed in Carreiro & Kapituik 2010. It has also been used in financial education, Shanklin & Ellen 2007, Campbell 2016. Vohs et.al. 2006 looks at the psychological effect of *Monopoly* money.

33   Banner 1998, 4

34   See for example patent US 1161984 filed by J.R Scott in 1915, or US 148270802 by E.W. Small in 1921, both of which show the spinner design discussed here.

35   Research is summarised in Groot et.al. 2004.

36   Galbraith 1954, 174.

37   For a general history of the VOC in English see Stevens & Pers, 1998.

38   Neal 2011, 314 quotes a letter from 1814 to this effect.

39   On the expansion of US share ownership see O'Sullivan 2007.

40   In 1930 members of the London exchange were banned from allowing outsiders to participate in their sweepstake and in 1931 their market in election results, which looked a lot like gambling, was shut down Beers, L.D. (2010) 'Punting on the Thames: Electoral Betting in Interwar Britain' Journal of Contemporary History, vol.45, no.2, 282-314.

41   It is unclear exactly when this idea was first developed, *Stock Exchange* a game reportedly published in 1929 may be the earliest example (see BGG 161618).

42   SEC Histories (Pickard 2009, 31). The Securities and Exchange Commission Historical Society, http://www.sechistorical.org/museum/oral-histories/, maintains an oral history archive consisting of interviews with staff. In this chapter they are referenced with the surname of the interviewee and year of interview.

43   In the 1909 Strong v Repide case, https://supreme.justia.com/cases/federal/us/213/419/, the court ruled "A director upon whose action the value of the shares depends cannot avail of his knowledge of what his own action will be to acquire shares from those whom he intentionally keeps in ignorance of his own action and the resulting value of the shares".

44   See the SEC historical website article "Fair to all people", http://www.sechistorical.org/museum/galleries/it/takeCommand_b.php

45   SEC histories (Fedders, 2006, 2-3)

46   SEC histories (Lynch 2006) recalls of the legal set-backs in the Chiarella case "After Chiarella, it wasn't enough just merely to show that the trader possessed insider information… When Chiarella came in, it didn't take long to develop the misappropriation theory which became the central". See also SEC histories (Levine 2006, 8-9)

47   SEC History (Lynch, 2006: 18).

48   Patrick 1972.

49   Manne 1966.

50   Mahoney 2003, and Moore 2012.

51   Blum 1986.

52   Ollman 1983, 18, lists *Ratrace* among several games that 'positively exalt all that is vile'.

53   Parlett 2007.

54   https://board gamegeek.com/thread/106869/review-stockmarket

55   As explained in the accompanying booklet stock market buying and selling depends to some degree on verbal agreements, the origin of this phrase.

56   Ollman 1983,167.

57   For a discussion of the publication date of the game see Huber 2014.

58   Levy & Weingartner 1990, 251.

59   Sackson 1969, 162. Note that other than being unaware that Charles Darrow did not introduce the coloured groupings of properties Sackson's remarks are identical in both the first edition of 1969 and subsequent editions.

60   He won the Spiel de Jahre once in 1981 for *Focus*, originally published in 1964, which is an abstract strategy game more akin to traditional games like *Draughts* or *Reversi*.

61   Dice usually produce independent probabilities (no matter how unlucky you get your odds of rolling a 1 on the next roll are unaltered) while cards tend to produce dependent probabilities (if you draw a 6 card there is one less 6 card in the deck to be drawn on a subsequent turn).

62   Ollman 1983, 267-74; Steiner & Rosenbaum 1979; Brown 1979.

63   Extract from a poem by Christopher Anstey published in 1780, quoted in Banner 1998, 89.

64   Banner 1998, 97.

65   This advice appears on page 14 of the rule book in the introduction to 'The Full Game'

66   SEC Oral Histories (Donahue, 2011, 10-11).

67   Lewis 2008 draws a direct line between Black Monday in 1987 and the financial crash in 2008.

68   Strange 1986.

69   Cassidy 2009, 13.

70   Galbraith 1954, 26.

71   An interesting aspect of this is the degree to which players tend to treat games as accurate depictions of how stock markets work. Though it might be argued that punt, insider, investor, and crash games all capture some essential essence

none of them reproduces even remotely accurately the actual details of stock markets. For example, see the review by user Rich Furst, 22 Jul 2011, https://board gamegeek.com/thread/678011/black-friday-not-about-propabilities-its-about-beh, which treats the game as an accurate representation.

72   McKibbin 1979, 173.

73   Letter to the Home Secretary, 1906, in Laybourn, 2017.

74   Letter 29 Dec 1937, to W.Lee & R.V.Palmer, WYC1163/box 13.

75   Parker Brothers had been asked for permission to use the name when the game was first published but for whatever reason this was either not received or not recalled by the chief executive in 1950 when he wrote asking for it to be discontinued (R.B.M Barton to N.Watson WYL1164/1). Waddingtons offered to discontinue the name which Parker Brothers initially accepted though the game carried on being published. The lack of extended conflict likely resulted from the very cordial relationship revealed in the extensive correspondence between the heads of the two companies.

76   The drawings in the patents for *Totopoly* show a banknote design identical with that in *Monopoly*, likely because the designers had used *Monopoly* money in their prototypes.

77   WYC 1164/13 Note appended by Victor Watson to a copy sent to Parker Brothers.

79   Inexperience may also have played a part. In 1938 Waddingtons were still primarily a printers with limited practical experience of board games, before licensing *Monopoly* from Parker Brothers its only games had been based on its prior experience as a producer of cards, *Beaver* in 1932, *Lexicon* in 1932. See Chartres, 1993, 157 – 161.

80   Acton 1990.

81   It is a common trope on the internet, see for example https://www.doyouremember.co.uk/memory/totopoly.

82   WYC1164/13, Walter Lee had died at the age of 90 in 1965 and from that point as per the original agreement his royalties were paid to his daughters.

83   The agreement, preserved in the archives of the company, appears to suggest to a lay person like the author that the company would give up its rights to the game if it ceased to pay royalties. Several letters from one of the designers indicate he had also understood it in this way.

84   By 1968 Waddington's lawyers were advising the company to play up Parker Brothers fears about the robustness of its claim on *Monopoly* as a negotiating strategy.

85   The quote is from the editorial of the second issue of *Gamers International*, without a by-line though Brian Walker was the editor at the time.

86   *Follyfoot* was based on a popular television series that ran from 1971 to 1974 in the UK which was based on a book, *Cobbler's Dream*, by Monica Dickens, the great granddaughter of Charles Dickens.

87   Parlett 2007.

88   Donovan 2017, 158.

89   *Smuggle* is the MB name for *Contraband*, a game originally produced by Pepys games in the UK during the late 1950s and early 1960s. It is loosely based on the traditional dice game, *Liar's Dice*.

90   Parlett 2007.

91   Levy & Weingartner 1990, 166.

92   Woods 2012, 18.

93   Fatsis 2002.

94   Erasmus 1950, 128.

95   Catalogues of 50s and 60s games demonstrate the extent to which thematic variations on established games dominated the American children's market, see Polizzi & Schaefer 1991.

96   See for example Larimore 2012.

97   A discussion of the Forbes rich list was published by Noer 2012, but the debate by economists was initially sparked by a short blog post by Bloomfield 2012, which produced responses by Woolley 2012, and Crampton 2012. The most detailed response by E-Crunch Ltd 2014 gave both the most detailed analysis and also the argument for a connection between the death of Smaug and the rise of Sauron.

98   The word 'money' is used in connection with the construction of Bag End, Bilbo's reaction to requests to borrow it, when Thorin talks of the mountain before Smaug's arrival, and when Bilbo leaves the Shire 'without a hat, a walking stick, or any money'; 'cash' is used only in connection with the contract offered to Bilbo at this time (all in An Unexpected Party); and 'coin' only in connection with the Trolls (Roast Mutton). 'Money' is mentioned a few times during the adventure, in reference to Dwarves 'being calculating folk' when they arrive at the mountain (Inside Information), 'money-counters' are mentioned by the people of Lake Town and 'Moneybags' used as an insult after Bard kills Smaug (Fire and Water). Though money is not used, the words 'sale' and 'auction' (The Last Stage) clearly imply it once Biblo returns to the Shire.

99   These episodes can be thought of as thresholds in the terminology of Joseph Campbell's *Hero with a Thousand Faces*. The applicability of Campbell's thesis to Tolkien in part because both are drawing on the same pool of European myths.

100   Rateliff 2007 511 and note 31

101   Tolkien, 1996 45, Doc.F2.

102   The only other reference to coins outside the Shire which otherwise survived in the novels is in Appendix A of *The Lord of the Rings* where in discussing Durin's Folk Tolkien refers to 'a few coins of little worth' in a purse thrown by the orcs of Moria.

103   Tolkien did accompany the original book with an illustration A Conversation with Smaug in which the dragon is depicted on a pile of gold. Some of the contents are clearly goblets and other such items but it is possible to imagine coins are intended.

104   The advert was run in prime time slots in both the USA (https://www.youtube.com/watch?v=wC2QJa8olUk) and the UK (https://www.youtube.com/watch?v=FY_YRatOInA) "Hero Quest. Deep inside another dimension face battling Barbarian and evil magic on a quest for adventure in a maze of monsters. This is Hero Quest, the fantasy adventure game where winning means mastering the arts of combat ("I'll use my broadsword") and magic ("Fire of wrath"). [Discover traps and enemies, uncover secret doors]. Once you get into it you will never be the same." Added in the UK "Now with two new adventure packs, the legend grows".

105   Platinum and electrum also feature in some versions.

106   Gold, silver, and copper, are separated by a factor of 100 rather than 10, for more details see https://wow.gamepedia.com/Money

107   Newspaper articles began to appear in the early 2000s suggesting various virtual economies were larger than most national economies, http://news.bbc.co.uk/1/hi/sci/tech/1899420.stm. In reality it is quite hard to measure but interested readers should look at the work of Edward Casronova, Castronova 2014, chapter 1; Lehdonvirta & Castronova, 2014, 149ff.

108   Noer 2012.

109   The opening line of a review for *6-Tage Rennen*, in *Games International* 1, 7.

110   Walker 1988, 30.

111   The lack of penetration of the Spiel de Jahre outside of Germany at this time is clear from Greenwood's misunderstanding, Kremlin was nominated in 1987 but did not win the award.

112   Wittgenstein 1953, #68.

113   When Wittgenstein's remarks are engaged with by gamers, see for example Costikyan 2011, 179, they are frequently misunderstood. Wittgenstein was not suggesting that you cannot define a word like 'game', but that bounded definitions of common characteristics are not in fact how words are used in the real-world. So you cannot produce the type of definition philosophers, or

in fact any sort of academic, uses and expect it to align with how the word is used. For example, in the hobby *Settlers of Catan* is often described as a euro-game but it shares almost none of the characteristics common to those games – it was simply a popular game by a German designer in the period when most successful games were euro-games. Any definition which included *Catan* would be worthless as an analytic tool, but it was called euro-game, and trying to impose either the popular usage on our analysis or thinking the analytic usage renders those real-world uses incorrect are both the sort of errors Wittgenstein was warning against.

114   The period from 1996 to 2008 is particularly important, especially in terms of reception. The winners of the Spiel de Jahre in this period, with the exception of a dexterity game, *Villa Palletti* in 2002, could all be described as euro-games. The period is bracketed by two winners based on distinctly different influences. *Settlers of Catan* in 1995, based on *Monopoly*, and *Dominion* in 2009 on American collectible card games such as *Magic: The Gathering*.

115   Though Woods 2012, 111ff, largely missies this they do correctly note that euro-games also tend to favour presenting randomness as something a player must respond to rather than something which resolves their actions. Mayer & Harris 2010, 4-5, misunderstand the change assuming that the games have a greater level of skill (describing one game with random elements incorrectly), a misunderstanding also apparent in Borit et.al. 2018. Though not true, the perception that euro-games involved less luck (rather than different sorts of luck) led to a trend to significantly reduce random elements in many subsequent games. A good example of this would be the critically successful *Puerto Rico*, published in 2002 late in the ascendency of the euro-game, which restricts its random element exclusively to the order in which plantations appear.

116   These games include *Hare & Tortoise* (1979), *Enchanted Forest* (1982), *Railway Rivals* (1984), *Top Secret Spies* (1986), *Auf Achse* (1987), *Barbarossa* (1988), *Um Reifenbreite* (1992), *Call my Bluff* (1993), and *The Settlers of Catan* (1995).

117   Online Review of *Power Grid* Joshua Noa, 13 Nov 2006, https://board gamegeek.com/article/1171641#1171641

118   Review by User Fawkes https://board gamegeek.com/article/59065# 59065, 11 Oct 2004

119   Charles Hasegawa 1 Mar 2006, https://board gamegeek.com/article/ 823935#823935

120   Woods 2012, 117, gives component quality as part of the definition of a euro-game.

121   Campbell 2018.

122   Boeschoten & Fas 1989, 320, found German preferences in the 80s unremarkable, though by the early 2000s the weak uptake of credit cards had become noticeable, see Harrison-Walker 2002, 13.

123 Mackintosh 2014. The publishers of the book, Penguin, have excerpted elements of this review on the back of the copy to make it sound much more positive than it actually was.

124 Rickards 2015, 217.

125 Rickards 2015, 239-40, uses the 18,000 figure. He also includes a disingenuous argument that critics who claim there is insufficient gold in the world are wrong because absolute quantities are irrelevant to a standard. While this is true of a standard it is not true of coins, which he conflates. The smallest pre-modern coins are those issued in Nepal sometimes known as 'whisps of wind' which can weigh as little as a hundredth of a gram. These are already so small as to have been impractical but on Rickards' estimates it would be necessary for a gold dollar coin to weight even less, a thousandth of a gram. Since that cannot be used in practice it places an immediate block on convertibility, with most users having to employ paper money even under a gold standard.

126 Hockenhull 2015.

127 Rickards 2015, 220.

128 Notable exceptions include silk and salt.

129 Jones 2017.

130 Interview with Dirk Henn for a Kickstarter for the 'designer edition' https://www.kickstarter.com/projects/1082720051/alhambra-designers-edition/posts/2195671

131 A cast of the seal, from the city of Dijon, was moved in the 1970s to the British Library. All of the objects are mass-produced, and the Marinid double dinar is common enough you might expect to find it any substantial museum collection, but the seal, the particular Iranian coin (an unusual gold rather than a common silver coin of Khusro II), and the lead medal, are all relatively unusual items.

132 For example the famous designer Reiner Knizia received a PhD in mathematics from Ulm in 1986.

133 The game rule which is not discussed here is that a player who buys with exact change is permitted to take an additional action. That action could then be used to take another currency card, which would effectively be a discount on the purchase. It Is this discount which makes the 6, 7, or 8, all of which pay exactly for more cards and work in more combination than the 9, more valuable.

134 Chris Wray 'SdJ Re-Reviews #25: Alhambra' https://opinionatedgamers.com/2015/10/31/sdj-re-reviews-25-alhambra/, 2015; see also the critical review Kyle Smith, 'Alhambra Review' in The Critical Gamer, June 16 2013 http://criticalboard gamer.blogspot.co.uk/2013/06/alhambra-review.html or

Molly Ellis, 2013 'Alhambra – A Surpising Spiel de Jahres Winner' http://www. gameparadisestore.com/wordpress/alhambra-a-surprising-spiel-de-jahres-winner/

135   Sicart 2014, 2

136   Barton & Somerville 2012, 68.

137   The games are outlined at her personal website Romero, B. http://brenda. games/work-1/; at the time of writing *Train* is the only one of the games in the series to have an entry on the database site Board Game Geek (BGG 63933).

138   The first two games are *The New World* and *Siochan Leat, "The Irish Game"*.

139   That the argument is aimed at those interested in video games is indicated by Romero's own background as a video-game designer, but also by the fact that the overwhelming academic response occurs in contexts otherwise dedicated to video games, so Logas 2011 and Deterding 2015 both occur in proceedings on digital games, Braithwaite & Sharp 2010, Swain 2010, Sharp, 2015, in volumes otherwise concerned with digital games, and when it is rarely included amongst board games, as in Ferrari 2011 work, it is by a researcher who works with digital games.

140   In a talk http://brenda.games/speaking/ 34:25.

141   Logas 2011 raises an interesting exception in which this question does arise. She points out that players who successfully identify the theme from the context will often continue to play without telling the other players, obeying a 'meta-rule' not to 'spoil' it for other players – though apparently they attempt to sabotage the other players, again suggesting they would only aid the system when they were unaware of where the trains were going.

142   This was the basis of a critical review on the Board Game Geek site by user Darilian which led to a lengthy debate which will be quoted from in this section https://boardgamegeek.com/thread/572773/train-historical-game-no-sense-historical-truth.

143   User ajoer 11 Oct 2010 https://boardgamegeek.com/thread/572773/train-historical-game-no-sense-historical-truth

144   The image shows wooden pawns of various sizes tightly packed into a container without spaces in a way that could be compared with *Tetris* the game which inspired the level in *Playing History 2*.

145   Talk http://brenda.games/speaking/ 8:54 includes remarks 'tragically boring board games', 'our culture does not have the best history of producing really compelling board games that engage the entire family' accompanied by a slide depicting *Monopoly* which suggest she is reproducing common attitudes from contemporary gamers rather than an understanding of the history of American board games before the advent of euro-games.

146   User fellonmyhead, 27 Apr 2004, https://boardgamegeek.com/thread/20052/

why-game-should-definitely-be-deleted, a number of other users echo similar sentiments.

147 Desatoff 2017.

148 The original German is published on https://www.spiel-des-jahres.com/ de/puerto-rico, "Siedler machen neue Felder urbar, der Bürgermeister teilt den Spielenden Kolonisten zu, die - vom Aufseher zur Arbeit angetrieben – entsprechend Waren produzieren. Der Baumeister wiederum errichtet die für die Produktion benötigten Gebäude. Für die Waren bekommt man beim Händler Geld, während der Kapitän die Waren nach Europa verschifft, wofür es schließlich Siegpunkte gibt."

149 Borit et.al. 2018 is mostly concerned with applying academic theories of colonialism and becomes confused over the issue of slavery, initially recognising the 'colonists' are clearly slaves, 14-15, but subsequently disingenuously stating 'the world is populated only by colonists who arrive from the metropolitan centres by ship', 23.

150 In interviews Seyfarth has made clear that he always begins with and develops the game around its theme, in 2005 https://boardgamegeek.com/thread/97046/ interviews-optimist-87-andreas-seyfarth-puerto-ri, and in 2010 http:// brettspillguiden.no/interview-with-andreas-seyfarth-2/.

151 Threads discussing the issue on the site can be found in 2003 https:// www.boardgamegeek.com/article/6845, https://boardgamegeek.com/ thread/16395/colonizing-ideal-world, 2004 https://boardgamegeek.com/ thread/ 21737/racial-overtones-pr-and-black-gamers, and 2007 https:// boardgamegeek.com/thread/149285/help-w-discussion-questions.

152 See Borit. et.al. 2018, 28 and note, subsequent notes here for Mayer and Harris 2010, and the preface to Woods 2012. These academics also tend to be specifically players who adopted the hobby in the wake of the euro-game explosion and associate their identity specifically with those games. Though there is insufficient material to really describe this as a field of study it can only be hoped that as it expands it will attract interest from academics who do not share this perspective and can offer the diversity of experience and background which is necessary for a healthy field.

153 Mayer & Harris 2010, 11, for the authentic game experience argument, 110, *Power Grid* and, 55, *Puerto Rico*. The book, 65, confirms the authors are gamers and likely adopting an insider perspective.

154 From the Designer's Notes of the English rules.

155 See http://scottnicholson.com/pubs/index.html for his writings.

156 This line is the last sentence in the introductory text so thematically frames the game.

157 Banner 1998 discusses this in his first chapter on English attitudes to trading.

158 Galbraith, 1957, 27-8, argues that this common explanation of crashes shows

a weak understanding of historical processes. Campbell & Turner 2012 suggest that crashes tend to impact experienced as well as inexperience investors.

159   At 21:20 in his podcast, Board Games with Scott, episode 61, https://www. youtube.com/watch?v=Q-Oz4y8HhI4

160   Qureshi, 2018.

161   In personal correspondence the designer was unable to offer an example of a RoSCA which operated on lowest bids, in which previous pot winners benefited from subsequent bids, or in which the number of rounds was such that players would benefit an unequal number of times (which happens with other than four or eight players).

162   See for example BGG 125879 for an early game to which this label was applied.

163   The first of a series of very lengthy threads began in the forums of Board Game Geek on this subject in 2013 'Are semi-cooperative games flawed?' https://boardgamegeek.com/thread/981179/are-semi-co-op-games-flawed, shows the level of interest it attracts.

164   Hoffman 2017.

165   The first edition of Buccaneer was produced with an oil cloth board in a tube rather than the subsequent flat board (which was then subsequently shrunk altering the game play in late editions). Waddingtons seem to have had some difficulty sourcing parts and the war time break in production was much longer than for Totopoly, so these first editions are much rarer.

166   Valuations of £200-300 sometimes seen in the press seem to rest largely on sources in the trade attempting to drum up interest with gullible journalists (see for example https://www.thisismoney.co.uk/money/news/ article-3367091/Got-Buccaneer-attic-s-worth-booty-Classic-board-games-proving-shrewd-investment-selling-thousands.html). While you certainly could pay that if you wished, or were very impatient, in the year the author wrote this he had seen at least four different copies at various markets for under £20, and there were at least twenty examples on ebay for under £30 on the day this sentence was written.